Language and ideology in children's fiction

John Stephens

LONGMAN

LONDON AND NEW YORK

Longman Group UK Limited
Longman House, Burnt Mill,
Harlow, Essex CM20 2JE, England
and Associated Companies throughout the world.

*Published in the United States of America
by Longman Publishing, New York*

© Longman Group UK Limited 1992

First published 1992

British Library Cataloguing-in-Publication Data

A catalogue record for this book is available from the British Library

Library of Congress Cataloging-in-Publication Data

Stephens, John, 1944–
   Language and ideology in children's literature / John Stephens.
      p.   cm. -- (Language in social life series)
   Includes bibliographical references and index.
   ISBN 0–582–07063–5. -- ISBN 0–582–07062–7 (pbk.)
   1. Children's literature--History and criticism.   2. Ideology and
literature.   I. Title.   II. Series.
PN1009.A1S82 1992
809'.89282--dc20   91–29744
                                                              CIP

Typeset by 7V in 10pt palatino

Produced by Longman Singapore Publishers (Pte) Ltd.
Printed in Singapore

Contents

41-44

v

In memoriam

Marcella Ryan   Imogen Stephens

General Editor's Preface

Central to the identity of the *Language in Social Life* series is the concept of interdisciplinarity, not only in terms of subject-matter, but also of methodology. Through the books in the Series, readers are being asked to make use of their intimate knowledge of language in particular manifestations and contexts as a means of exploration, of disciplinary fields, of social theories and social structures, of their own positions in relation to those fields and to their societies, and of the place language plays in such an exploration. In sum, readers are being asked to engage in a dialectic process between the text of particular discourses and their own subjectivities, drawing on a range of reading strategies to explore often unfamiliar social worlds. Language in such an engagement is more than merely world-reflecting; rather text and its discourses are seen as constitutive of particular social worlds, as much determining as determined. Through exploring language in this critical way, readers can find their own subjectivities challenged as they engage with what John Stephens in this imaginative and innovative study of children's fiction calls the *polyphony* of discourse.

Literature written for children is, of course, a magnificent vehicle for monitoring and exploring this positioning and engagement of the reader, and for a variety of reasons. As John Stephens illustrates clearly, it makes necessary a broadening of a surface author-reader relationship to encompass a complex of implied authors, narrators, narratees, and implied readers, which is significant for the understanding of reading in general, not merely of texts for children. Moreover, the complexity is not just a matter of the participants in the writing-reading process, it lies also in the richness of such texts where intertextuality is raised to a guiding authorial principle, the unpacking of whose examples offers insights to the careful reader into current sociolinguistic convention, into active social and moral struggles and their representation in contemporary cultural forms. Readers will notice how in his exploration of what he terms the 'carnivalesque', John Stephens demonstrates how children's fiction parodies and mocks these recognizable social forms and moral positions. Indeed, the very richness of textual structure in children's fiction, its by no means 'simple' language, has the effect as this book points out, not only of socialising Goodman's psycholinguistic 'guessing game' but in doing so making conscious how adults and children variously go about the reading process, and how their naturalised social values and ideologies are reinforced or, much less often, challenged.

It would be quite wrong, however, to see this book merely in terms of a vehicle for the exploration of relationships between language and social life, if, as it were, the author had simply selected a convenient genre for a discourse on social theory or for a treatment of admittedly acute issues of contemporary society, such as those of race, gender, class and power. *Language and Ideology in Children's Fiction* is in itself an innovative and original contribution to the study of children's literature. It offers its readership a brightly illustrated typology of the range of genres the field subsumes and discusses *inter alia* the place of visualisation and semiotics, the contemporary relevance of the defamiliarising historicity common to many texts constructed for children and the value of a critical linguistic analysis in the understanding of textual imagery and tale. The book has, however, a relevance beyond that merely of the understanding of children's literary texts to the study of the language of fiction more generally. John Stephens makes the case, for example, that with one or two pioneering exceptions, there has still been little influential application of pragmatics to the critical understanding of literary texts, and hardly any at all of the contribution of research into conversational structure to such an understanding. Furthermore, contemporary sociolinguistic attention to the relationships of language to social and personal power, in the sense of the critical explanation of unequal encounters, has found little resonance in literary critical discussion. This is unfortunate given the engagement of fiction with human life and its discourses and the attention paid by critics to author-character-narrator-reader relationships. I am thinking here not only of the original relationships drawn in this book between the various types of carnivalesque children's texts and, following Bakhtin, their socially interrogative functions, but even more the careful distinction drawn between metonymic and metaphoric modes in John Stephens' quite original discussion of fantasy and realism in children's fiction. Indeed, it is one of the prime contributions of this book to the canon of literary criticism that it demonstrates through its example texts and text-types how literary forms can offer exemplary evidence for the ways individuals, whether fictional characters or subjects in real life, see events, objects, persons and activities from undisclosed and naturalised positions and how children's fictional texts are engaged, as the author puts it, in a struggle for young people's minds. In this way, too, children's fiction becomes a means for an historical understanding of how, at different periods, particularistic sociocultural values dominate through being accorded the status of universal significance.

As with other contributions to the *Language in Social Life* series, this book has been deliberately constructed to afford the opportunity of reader engagement and debate. Its style is intentionally issue-raising and challenging, and the author's inclusion of the *Taking It Further* sections in the various chapters has been explicitly designed to stimulate both seminar discussion, if appropriate, and personal research. Carefully selected *Further Readings* support this research process, guiding the reader both to the specialist literature and to more general works in the spirit of interdisciplinarity which this Preface has emphasised.

In summary and in one telling phrase, John Stephens explores here the *'words of power'*, and in doing so through the perhaps unaccustomed genre of children's fiction, displays for a broader readership than the merely literary, how all stories achieve social significance.

Professor Christopher N Candlin
Macquarie University, Sydney

Author's Acknowledgements

I would like to thank Chris Candlin for suggesting this project to me and then for reading the manuscript with an astute eye both for its flaws and its possibilities. I have no doubt it is a better book for his encouragement and care. I also owe a special debt to Robyn McCallum, who not only helped me assemble material and talked through much of the secondary literature with me, but was also that important person every author needs – the supportive colleague who believes in the ultimate virtue of the project. Margaret Bartholomew and Gwen Griffiths also read versions of the manuscript with keen attention and healthy scepticism, and suggested many necessary improvements. Finally, Kathryn Gresham, formerly of the Curriculum Resources Centre of Macquarie University Library, supplied me with a constant stream of pertinent information while I was researching the book, and was always ready to offer a teacher–librarian's perspective on my work. If, however, I have made grievous omissions, or sometimes fail to make sense, it is my own fault and not the fault of these friends and colleagues.

The opening section of Chapter 3 appeared in a different form and context in *Children's Literature in Education*. Part of Chapter 2 was presented as a lecture to The Family Therapy Association of NSW.

Publisher's Acknowledgements

We are grateful to the following for permission to reproduce copyright material:

the author's agent for an extract from 'Little Red Riding Hood and the Wolf' from *Revolting Rhymes* by Roald Dahl (Jonathan Cape, 1982 and Penguin Books, 1984); Victor Gollancz & Viking Penguin, a division of Penguin Books USA Inc. for extracts from *Fun* by Jan Mark, illustrated by Michael Foreman. Copyright © 1987 by Jan Mark for text. Copyright © 1987 by Michael Foreman for illustrations; the author's agent for the poem 'Hide and Seek' from *Nailing the Shadow* by Roger McGough (Penguin Books, 1989); the editor's agent for two rhymes from *Cinderella Dressed in Yella* edited by Ian Turner, June Factor and Wendy Lowenstein; Methuen Childrens Books, L. Garfield and M. Bragg for PLATE 1 from *The Writing on the Wall*; Murdoch Books of North Sydney, Australia for PLATE 2 from *A New Coat for Spikey* by Janet Slater and Steve Dickinson; Penguin Books Australia Ltd, Jenny Wagner and Jeff Fisher for PLATE 3 from *The Machine at the Heart of the World* story Jenny Wagner, illustrations Jeff Fisher; Hamish Hamilton Ltd. and The Putnam Publishing Group, New York, for PLATE 4 from *Prince Cinders* by Babette Cole, copyright © 1987 by Babette Cole; Walker Books Ltd and Alfred A. Knopf, Inc, for PLATE 5, from *Willy the Wimp* © 1984 Anthony Browne; Penguin Books Ltd, the author and the illustrator's agents for illustration, PLATE 6, and text, from *Out of the Oven* by Jan Mark and Anthony Maitland (Viking Kestral, 1986) copyright © Jan Mark, 1986, illustrations copyright © Anthony Maitland, 1986; Faber and Faber Ltd (Publishers) and HarperCollins publishers for PLATE 7 from *A Baby Sister for Frances* by Russell Hoban, illustrated by Lillian Hoban. Illustration copyright © Lillian Hoban; Walker Books Limited and Alfred A. Knopf, Inc. for PLATE

INTRODUCTION

Examining ideology in children's fiction

> Culture is an historical process of human objectification, and the level and quality of a national culture depends on the socialization developed by human beings to integrate young members into the society and to re-inforce the norms and values which legitimise the sociopolitical system and which guarantee some sort of continuity in society.
>
> (Jack Zipes 1983, p. 54)

A major aspect of intellectual thought during the last three or four decades has been the recognition of the importance of the critical study of language for any understanding of social life. This awareness applies generally to attempts to understand the ideological practices and assumptions which determine a society's sense of meaning and value, and it applies particularly to how individual selfhood is constructed, and to what mechanisms govern interpersonal relationships and social hierarchies. It has been argued from a number of social and critical perspectives that language as a system of signification – what is commonly referred to as *discourse* – is endemically and pervasively imbued with ideology (Barthes 1972; Larrain 1979; Fairclough 1989). My present concern with ideology does not aim to encompass discourse as social practice in its widest applications. This area has already been ably examined by the first book in this series, Norman Fairclough's *Language and Power* (1989), which I have drawn upon in my early chapters. Rather, I am concerned here with that more specific discourse of narrative fiction produced for children aged between infancy and early adolescence. While multiple and diverse in itself, this discourse is nevertheless quite specialized, and in order to analyse the workings of ideological practices within it I have formulated a new interdisciplinary methodology which combines several preoccupations and insights of contemporary critical linguistics and literary theory and practice.

As with discourse in general, the discourses of children's fiction

1

are pervaded by ideological presuppositions, sometimes obtrusive-ly and sometimes invisibly. Their presence may be thought of as analogous to a geometrical shape in which one figure is inscribed within another, as an octagon within a square, for example, in such a way that the two figures merge at overlapping boundaries. Seg-ments thus exist in which the inner figure coincides with the outer and becomes invisible (see Figure 1). Following this analogy, in sub-sequent discussion I will often use the term 'inscribed' to refer to the presence of ideology within discourse.

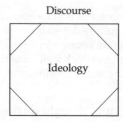

Discourse

Ideology

Figure 1 Discourse and ideology

The ideology of a text may at times be rendered obtrusively, as when segments of the octagon are separate from the square, but much of the time it is implicit. The geometrical model offers only a limited analogy, however, because in actual practice ideology is never separable from discourse. Its presence is only more or less ap-parent. I will argue in Chapter 1 that the discourse of a narrative fiction yields up both a *story* and a *significance*. Ideology may be in-scribed within both. On the one hand, the significance deduced from a text – its theme, moral, insight into behaviour, and so on – is never without an ideological dimension or connotation. On the other hand, and less overtly, ideology is implicit in the way the story an audience derives from a text exists as an isomorph of events in the actual world: even if the story's events are wholly or partly impossible in actuality, narrative sequences and character interrelationships will be shaped according to recognizable forms, and that shaping can in itself express ideology in so far as it implies assumptions about the forms of human existence. This is obvious, for example, in anthropomorphic picture books or folk tales in which animals are depicted performing social actions and functions particular to human beings, in that the discrepancy between human and animal behaviour can easily mask the assumption that the implied human behaviour reflects social reality. Stereotypical sexual, racial and class attitudes, with concomitant social practices, have long been implicitly inscribed in this way. Because ideology is thus present as an implicit secondary meaning at two levels, fiction must be regarded as a special site for ideological effect, with a potentially powerful capacity for shaping audience attitudes.

Writing for children is usually purposeful, its intention being to foster in the child reader a positive apperception of some socio-cultural values which, it is assumed, are shared by author and audience. These values include contemporary morality and ethics, a sense of what is valuable in the culture's past (what a particular contemporary social formation regards as the culture's centrally important traditions), and aspirations about the present and future. Since a culture's future is, to put it crudely, invested in its children, children's writers often take upon themselves the task of trying to mould audience attitudes into 'desirable' forms, which can mean either an attempt to perpetuate certain values or to resist socially dominant values which particular writers oppose. Such ideological positions are often quite overt, as when Louise Lawrence's nuclear holocaust fantasy, *Children of the Dust*, bears the dedication 'For the children that they may never know the dust', and thus proclaims itself as a modern cautionary tale. Often, such writers are concurring with or responding to attempts to change social practices and assumptions as expressed by significant groups within society – government, boards of education, ecology-orientated organizations, women's groups, and so on.

There are also less obvious social and ethical ideologies pervading children's fiction, and these inhere in the representations of relationships between the individual and society. Teachers see personal development and growth in self-understanding as major purposes for reading literature (Protherough 1983, p. 7), and this perception is mirrored in the fiction itself in a tendency for children's fiction to focus attention predominantly on the individual psyche. Arguably the most pervasive theme in children's fiction is the transition within the individual from infantile solipsism to maturing social awareness. This transition may open out into the larger social areas mentioned above, or it may be a more specific personal development, or it may be thwarted (I will later cite some recent discussions of popular junior fiction which have described some narratives that confuse personal development with extreme solipsism). But all developmental paths are ideologically constructed, involving conformity to societal norms, and it is important for anyone concerned with children's fiction to develop an awareness of the processes and ends of this construction. I have found it useful to draw on recent discussions of individual selfhood, or subjectivity, as it is now more generally called, in order to address this issue.

Behind most recent discussion of children's fiction lies Iser's observation that literature constructs a unique relationship between an observer and an object (1978, pp. 108–9). Iser argued that readers are situated inside a literary text, that the subject (the reader) is located inside the object (the narrative) it has to apprehend. Without even being applied too loosely, this view confirms a common assumption that a reader's subjectivity is effaced as part of the reading process. In Protherough's five-fold division of children's descriptions of what they do when they read (1983, pp. 20–5), all of the 'modes' involve total or near-total effacing of reader subjectivity. Only the fifth, 'Detached evaluation', involves a more critical reader stance, and Protherough regards this mode with some suspicion as 'a form of behaviour learned in school' (p. 24). Some ambivalence, at least, might be expected given Protherough's theoretical and practical commitment to a theory that gives pre-eminence to reader response. But must critical reading inevitably block individual response? Is individual response at the cost of reader subjectivity so uniquely valuable if its consequence is reader subjection to the ideologies of the text? I am openly polemical on this point, for I believe that if we consider the ideology of texts to be important then education systems in the English-speaking world often inculcate a defective model of reading. There are two sides to this problem. First, the importance of *verisimilitude* is overstated: a book 'based on a true story' is inherently preferable to a book which is a mere fiction; language which evokes 'the real world' is preferable to language which doesn't. The purpose here may be to orientate the child towards 'the real world', but its effect is to imply a one-to-one relationship between objects and their representation, and hence to mask the processes of textual production of meaning: representation becomes equated with 'truth'. Secondly, and connectedly, children are encouraged to situate themselves inside the text by identifying with a principal character and its construction and experience of the world. To put it bluntly, a mode of reading which locates the reader only within the text is disabling, and leaves readers susceptible to gross forms of intellectual manipulation. The problem is not only one of schooling, since the number of writers who write with such a reading process in mind is in the majority, and the same assumptions can be discerned in, for example, picture books and anthropomorphic animal stories. Finally, as Rose (1984) and others have pointed out, many writers and authorities in the field of children's fiction have had a stake in promoting this situation as a defence against what they perceive as the cultural threat of modernism.

A critical methodology able to examine the interrelated issues of the ideologies of texts and the subjectivity of readers will need to incorporate both critical linguistics and aspects of modern theories of narrative. The critical study of *language* is central to the methodology, since it is through language that the subject and the world are represented in literature, and through language that literature seeks to define the relationships between child and culture. Hence fiction produced for children is an important area for discourse analysis, in order to disclose the processes and effects of those representations and definitions. At the same time, though, the discourses of fiction incorporate crucial features not normally present in actual spoken discourse, and unless these are included in the critical methodology analysis will proceed on wrong premises. An interview between unequals, for example, may have a dynamic comparable to those analysed by Thomas (1985), but now becomes an artful construct framed by a narrating voice, able to switch between direct and indirect speech representation, and requiring to be read for intentional thematic and ideological significances as well as for its dramatic depiction of language as a mechanism of social power. It is to the detriment of the study of children's fiction that such analysis has not been attempted on any significant scale. There are, for example, substantial linguistic and narrative studies of stories produced *by* children, but there is an absence of equivalent studies of fiction produced *for* them. Further, there exists no substantial attempt to examine fiction written for children by bringing together into one methodology the elements of narrative theory, critical linguistics, and a concern with ideology and subjectivity. My aim in this book is to fill that gap, examining narrative fictions of various kinds and genres produced for children up to about their eighth year of school.

As an anticipation of and a guide to how I have gone about my aim, a summary of chapter contents follows. It should be noted that wherever cited I have given the pictures in picture books at least the same status as signifying systems as that ascribed to systems of language, and in some cases greater status.

Chapter 1 lays the ground for an examination of ideology by expounding a theory of narrative. It argues that narrative discourse must be read as a linguistic and a narratological process, and for both its story and its significance; that readers construct significance by a diversity of reading processes; that narrative structure is an ideologically powerful component of texts; and that narrative discourse enables a range of possible reader subject positions.

Chapter 2 is concerned with some strategies by which readers may be prevented from adopting a singular subject position. It argues that the relationship between a reader (as subject) and a narrative fiction (as object) mirrors other forms of subject/sociality interactions, so that the creation of characters as intersubjective constructs functions as a model for the construction of reader subjectivity. The ideological impact of a text on its readers varies according to the possible interpretative subject positions; the *subject* can signify not only the role of one who acts, but also one who is *subjected* to the authority of the text. The interaction of discourse types draws attention to narrative processes, so that subject positions may be evaluated; the meaning of a text may also be constituted as a dialectic between textual discourse and a reader's pre-existing subjectivity. Finally, the concept of focalization is shown to be crucial to the analysis of subjectivity and ideology in narrative fictions.

Chapter 3 examines the relationship between intertextuality and ideology. Meaning is produced by the interconnections of discourse and society, an observation of great importance to children's fiction which has no discourse of its own, but is an amalgam of other discourses, including broadly defined cultural discourse. Intertextuality encourages self-conscious subjectivity because it is structurally similar to intersubjectivity, because it keeps visible the processes of narrative discourse and representation, and because its play of differences functions as a critique of social values.

Chapter 4 examines a special kind of intertextual mode: carnivalesque interrogative. Based on the premise that what is socially desirable and socially undesirable are cultural and linguistic constructs, such texts temporarily or radically evade, invert or transgress ideologies and structures of authority. By denying simple empathy with characters or situations, and by emphasizing signifying processes, such narratives situate readers outside the text as separate subjects.

Chapter 5 deals with representations of reality and socialization in picture books. Learning how to read a picture book is itself a socializing process heavily imbued with ideological assumptions about the nature of existence and reality. The pervasive concern with self–other interactions in picture books has considerable implications for the construction of subjectivity, but operates in contexts which tend to encourage the internalization of ideologies which are commonly a reflection of dominant social practices. The representation of power relationships in conversational exchanges often figures prominently and promotes the socialization of children into conventional roles.

Chapter 6 examines the ideological motivations of historical fiction, especially in the impulse to use the past to inculcate moral, humanist values, and to assert that human nature is stable and unchanging. To do this, writers make use of the discoursal conventions of realism, extended in such a way as to incorporate conventions for representing archaic speech without drawing attention to the textuality of the fiction. In works which encourage simple empathy there is a tendency to construct exemplary models and to refashion the past according to the values of the present. Works which demand more complex reading strategies, however, may suggest that causality and significance are imposed on the past retrospectively.

Chapter 7 argues that the distinction between fantasy and realism (perhaps the single most important generic distinction in children's fiction) can be discerned as a difference between linguistically constituted discourse modes, whereby fantasy is essentially a metaphoric mode and realism a metonymic mode. The two discourses are centrally concerned with the theme of language and power but encode it in different ways: realistic fiction doing so particularly through conversational encounters and allusions to social practice, and fantasy through a mythic representation of transcendent meaning. The processes of representation are usually overt in fantasy but effaced in realism; a consequence is that the ideological dimension of fantasy is present as allegory, but rendered unobtrusive, while in realism it is situated at the level of events and disclosed by strategies of focalization. The chapter concludes with an extended study of ideological representation in a fantastic fiction by Diana Wynne Jones and a realistic fiction by Lois Lowry.

ONE

Ideology, discourse and narrative fiction

IDEOLOGY

This book is concerned with the operations of ideology in fiction produced for children. It is grounded on the premise that what this otherwise rather amorphous body of texts has in common is an impulse to intervene in the lives of children. That is, children's fiction belongs firmly within the domain of cultural practices which exist for the purpose of socializing their target audience. Childhood is seen as the crucial formative period in the life of a human being, the time for basic education about the nature of the world, how to live in it, how to relate to other people, what to believe, what and how to think – in general, the intention is to render the world intelligible. Such ideas as these are neither essential nor absolute in their constitution but are constructed within social practices, and the intelligibility which a society offers its children is a network of ideological positions, many of which are neither articulated nor recognized as being essentially ideological.

Ideologies, of course, are not necessarily undesirable, and in the sense of a system of beliefs by which we make sense of the world, social life would be impossible without them. If a child is to take part in society and act purposively within its structures, he or she will have to master the various signifying codes used by society to order itself. The principal code is language, since language is the most common form of social communication, and one particular use of language through which society seeks to exemplify and inculcate its current values and attitudes is the imagining and recording of stories. A narrative without an ideology is unthinkable: ideology is formulated in and by language, meanings within language are socially determined, and narratives are constructed out of language.

8

The use of story as an agent of socialization is a conscious and deliberate process. In practice it ranges from the didactic extremes of 'bibliotherapy', books which purport to help children confront and deal with specific problems in their lives (death of a close relative; parental separation; starting at school, etc.), to books with no obvious intent to be exemplary. Every book has an implicit ideology, nevertheless, usually in the form of assumed social structures and habits of thought. The second kind of book can be the more powerful vehicle for an ideology because implicit, and therefore invisible, ideological positions are invested with legitimacy through the implication that things are simply 'so'. Many books are ideological in both ways, since a conscious attempt to bring about change in attitude will be grounded in any number of contingent presuppositions about the individual, society, cognitive processes, and so on. Ideology, then, need not be a product of deliberate policy – an attempt to advocate or even impose particular socio-political attitudes – since it also reflects beliefs and assumptions of which the author is, or may be, unaware. For example, Jan Needle is a writer who is fiercely and consciously political, and overtly uses his narratives to confront abuse of power, sexism, racism, economic exploitation and social neglect, so his books constantly question ruling ideologies. Diana Wynne Jones, a very intelligent writer of absorbing fantasies, appears to have been consistently unaware for most of her career that her depiction of women already socialized into conventional female roles is pervasively sexist (and to some extent classist). I will consider the functioning of implicit ideologies at more length below, especially in discussing picture books in Chapter 5 and fantasy in Chapter 7.

Some of these ideas have been explored by Peter Hollindale in a very useful paper dealing with the operations of ideology in children's literature (Hollindale 1988), and the next part of my discussion is based on the three aspects of ideology identified by Hollindale.

First, ideology appears as an overt or explicit element in the text, disclosing the writer's social, political or moral beliefs. Books which openly advocate 'progressive' or 'enlightened' ideas belong to this category. Hollindale suggests that there are problems of representation for writers here, in that explicit advocacy tends to provoke reader resistance to the message, and at the same time it concedes that the advocated value or behaviour is still a minority social practice, whereas the ideal behaviour can be in effect muted if presented as though it were normal social practice. And the more covert the representation, the more it demands a reader who knows how to interpret a fiction. This demand is itself an ideological assumption, of course.

Hollindale's second category is 'passive ideology', that is, the implicit presence in the text of the writer's unexamined assumptions. He points out, quite rightly I believe, that although it takes sophisticated analytical ability to demonstrate the presence of such ideologies, they are probably more powerful in effect, since they consist of values taken for granted in the society that produces and consumes the text, including children. Almost no attention has been paid to this aspect of children's literature, largely because until recently it has been masked by critical concern and controversy about an issue with which it actually overlaps, the concept of an implied reader. This concept is widely used in discussions of children's fiction, generally in the form of a hypothetical reader derived from a text's own structures and 'situated in such a position that he can assemble the meaning toward which the perspectives of the text have guided him' (Iser 1978, p. 38). A clear example of how the concept of the implied reader distracts attention from the operations of ideology within texts is to be found in Aidan Chambers frequently reprinted paper, 'The Reader in the Book' (Chambers 1977; reprinted 1985). In section 8 Chambers discusses the function of gaps in narrative 'which the reader must fill before the meaning can be complete' (p. 46), gaps which include assumptions of 'beliefs, politics, social customs'. His description of a successful reading thus envisages the reader's internalization of the text's implicit ideologies. What Chambers presents as an empowering act of interpretation is just as likely to be a process of subjection. The construction of an active role for the reader, what is generally referred to as a 'subject position', is a crucial part of the reading process, and I will examine it in detail in Chapter 2. It is enough to say for now that the relationship between ideology and subject positions in children's literature is, up to the present time, almost totally unexamined (see Stephens 1990b).

Thirdly, Hollindale identifies ideology as inherent within language, which he broadly characterizes as 'the words, the rule-systems, the codes which constitute the text' (p. 14). He argues that this inherency of ideology in language works to suppress articulations of conflict and to restrict signification to the attitudes and interests of dominant social groups. This view coincides with that of Fairclough (1989, p. 88), who remarks that ideological struggle pre-eminently takes place in language. Fairclough goes on to point out that this is also a struggle *over* language, in the sense that language is not just a *site* of social struggle but also an object of struggle, since an important aspect of social power lies in the power to determine word meanings and legitimate communicative norms. Hollindale suggests that if children can be made aware of how such ideologies operate in fictional representations they may be more empowered to identify equivalent ideological apparatuses in their experiences in the actual world. His paper is the most comprehensive exploration of ideology and children's literature so far published, but is rather limited in scope and methodology. More delicate analytical methods are needed to extend the analysis further, particularly methods which enable both finer linguistic evaluations and more sophisticated narratological insights. Such methods already exist, and I hope in this book to bring them together. The linguistic encoding of ideology has been extensively examined by, for example, Birch (1989), Fairclough (1989) and Fowler (1981; 1986), and there is a very large literature on narrative – see, for example, Chatman (1978), Rimmon-Kenan (1983), Martin (1986) and Toolan (1988).

DISCOURSE

It happens that linguists and narratologists use the same crucial term to refer to the 'surface' of the texts they work with. This term is *discourse*. It is, to some extent, a conveniently loose term, and the two groups of analysts I referred to use it in different, though analogous, senses. I propose to use both senses, as appropriate, because it is a convenient term and, since the two uses share a focus on *how* something is being encoded, there is little risk of ambiguity. My subsequent discussion will thus be grounded in the following definitions of *discourse*:

(a) *Linguistic*: 'stretches of language perceived to be meaningful, unified, and purposive' (Cook 1989, p. 156). This usage is commonly employed to refer to discoursal actions in general and to specific discourse types, such as the discourse of parent–child conversational encounters.
(b) *Narratological*: the means by which a story and its significance are communicated (including temporal sequencing, focalization, and the narrator's relation to the story and the audience).

The term is again used with broader and more specific reference, ranging from narrative discourse to the discourse of fantasy or of historical fiction, for example.

I believe analysis able to comprehend discourse in both these senses offers a useful basis for any attempt to understand what might be called the 'mode of being' of a work of narrative fiction. By 'mode of being' I refer to the complex of factors which go to make up the meaning of a narrative: initially this is language, which, in books for children, frequently operates in conjunction with visual messages transmitted by illustrations; but on a wide scale meaning is influenced by the larger contexts of text and culture within which particular utterances acquire meaning. Within the text, particular micro-utterances are affected by the elements which join them together into larger structures. These are of interest at two levels. First, at the level of more specifically linguistic features, such as the grammatical and other ties which combine sentences together into larger units. Second, at the level of elements often considered to be the domain of a more 'literary' purpose – type of narrator, the implied reader who is constructed by the text, point of view, allusion and theme, for example – but which are inextricably bound up with discourse in some more precisely linguistic application. Outside the text exists the cultural context which determines the range of, for example, semantic options available at particular textual moments. We can only speak loosely of 'outside', though, since language does not merely reflect the world but is crucial to the very constitution of the world.

NARRATIVE DISCOURSE AND CHILDREN'S LITERATURE

A narrative consists of three interlocked components: the *discourse*; a *'story'* which is ascertained by an act of primary reading (reading for 'the sense'); and a *significance*, derived by secondary reading from the first two (see Stephens and Waterhouse 1990, pp. 8–10). There is no doubt that readers reach a broad consensus about the primary level, though even here retellings of the 'story' will vary in emphasis and selected detail. Consensus seems possible, though, because of common human experiences which render specific characters and situations recognizable, and because some signifiers are, simply, unproblematic. Indeterminacy enters with the secondary reading level. Here is a simple example, presented as a poem which recalls a recurrent childhood situation:

Hide and Seek

When I played as a kid
How I longed to be caught
But whenever I hid
Nobody sought.

(Roger McGough, 'Hide and Seek')

The title draws on a specialist vocabulary, that of childhood play, and indeed the occurrence of the verb 'played' in line one quickly confirms that specialization. As such, it constitutes a minor piece of specialized knowledge – that is, that the two verbs are not to be understood as a sequential string but as a compound name. Without this knowledge the poem's story would be much harder to grasp. It should also be noted that 'seek' is more likely to exist in a child's passive vocabulary than active (where 'look for' is more usual): here it is fossilized in the game's compound title. Furnished with this piece of 'world-knowledge', a reader can easily grasp the sense, and paraphrase it as something like, 'When the speaker played Hide and Seek as a child, he wanted to be caught, but nobody ever looked for him.' The sense is so obvious that paraphrase is hardly necessary, but what my version shows is something about the vocabulary of the original: my substitutions of 'child', 'wanted' and 'looked for' mark points of register variation or even overwording (the use of many signifiers with a heavy emotive loading). These foregrounded points impact on how a reader reads for significance. The first, 'kid', emphasizes the retrospective situation of the utterance; 'longed' invests the emotion described with considerable force (as well as emphasizing how the speaker's desire was contrary to the purpose of the game, a deviation which first pushes the reader towards a secondary reading); and 'sought', as the climax of the rhyme pattern, and in conjunction with 'hid', by transposing the verbs of the title/game into past tense forms takes apart the compound and insists on a fullness of meaning. Hence the poem describes moments of childhood anguish, produced by exclusion and isolation, heightened by their situation within what is normally considered cooperative play. But what this offers readers is not an event but a feeling, and this feeling will differ from one reader to another, from child to adult, according to how they experience(d) moments of social rejection and how they subjectively recall them. That is, the poem creates an emotional space which the reader can inhabit largely on his or her own terms, matching the emotion from personal experience. The process involved here can be described as the text's creation of a subject position for the reader, a concept which is of inestimable importance for reading literary texts, and especially for examining the possibility of ideological impact on readers.

For acts of interpretation, the problem area in the discourse/story/significance triad seems to be *significance*: narratives invariably have thematic purposes and functions, whether deliberately because they seek to inculcate something about life, or implicitly because no encoding of a story can be free of societal and/or ideological marking, but how is the move to the level of significance accomplished? Broadly speaking, there is conventionally an expectation that such a move has to be made, and the impact on textuality of such top-down discoursal elements as social practice, generic relationships and inscribed point of view make such a move mandatory. But elements such as these do not necessarily specify or clarify the processes by which readers arrive at the thematic import of particular discoursal representations of a story. To do this, I suggest, readers must also be capable of bottom-up interpretation, and so be able to decode language in both small and large units, and be sensitive to how what can be called micro-discourses and macro-discourses interact.

I think a useful starting-point for describing this interaction of top-down and bottom-up processes can be found in the definition of discourse I cited earlier from Guy Cook: that is, 'stretches of language perceived to be meaningful, unified, and purposive'. This definition would also appear to serve adequately for most literary works, if its terms and premises were appropriately expanded, just as they need to be expanded to make it an operative linguistic definition. The definition has five components of crucial implication for a critical discourse (to give 'discourse' another of its common applications), especially one concerned with children's literature.

The first component, 'stretches of language', draws attention to the diversity of signifying systems within books for children. I'm not going to dwell on the obvious, but 'language' has to be understood as comprehending not just a verbal text but also the following: illustrations, which may vary from the integral to the decorative; pictures which are an inextricable part of what a book communicates; picture books with no words at all; pictures which pop up and have movable parts, and which offer a hands-on encounter with the story, and sometimes visually disclose information present in neither text nor unhandled picture. Further, stretches of verbal text in themselves vary enormously in length. A folk tale can be recounted in a couple of hundred words, as, for example, Katherine Briggs' retelling of 'The Bogie's Field' (Briggs 1979, pp. 34–5); a thirty-two-page picture book can have 400 words or fewer, and even complex picture book texts often only extend to between 500 and 700 words. Conversely, a picture book such as Graham Oakley's *Henry's Quest* may be very detailed in both pictures and text, and then, over and above that intrinsic elaboration, link picture and text contrapuntally, thus offering a rich and complex reading experience. (A municipal librarian informant tells me the book was very popular with Australian children in years seven and eight.) Finally, novels for older readers can be 200 or 300 pages long and several of them, as in Cynthia Voigt's 'Tillerman' novels, may even be arranged in a sequence.

The second and third components, respectively, introduce into the field of discourse the issues of *perception* and of *power*. These are important issues here, first because they begin to move interpretation into the sphere of significance, and second because they highlight a tendency in narratological theories, derived as they were principally from structuralism, to consider these matters only as features intrinsic to the text. Critical linguistics, however, also addresses the extrinsic aspect, arguing that without this, intrinsic solutions are false constructions. If something is said to be '(a) perceived to be (b) meaningful', it raises the question of who does the perceiving and who determines meaningfulness. Communication presupposes at least two communicators, and fields of study such as functional grammar and pragmalinguistics have dealt extensively with the interpersonal functions of linguistic discourse. With literary texts, the study of intrinsic perceptions has been prominent since at least the publication of Wayne Booth's seminal *The Rhetoric of Fiction* (1961), but acceptance of the idea that readers have an active role in perception and the construction of meaning is recent. The intrinsic question 'Who sees?' is very important to analysis, and plays a large part in my own discussions here and elsewhere (see Stephens and Waterhouse 1985). Within the text it is a focus on the making of meaning, which may not be the same meaning as a reader perceives or makes, and that reader's perceptions and notions of meaningfulness are in their turn at least partly determined by the reader's own social context.

Components four and five of Cook's definition specify that discourse is perceived as 'unified' and 'purposive'. These again have crucial implications for the reading of literature, and especially for children's literature. Both lie essentially in the sphere of significance. The unity of a text is manifested tangibly in such elements as the ordering of spatio-temporal representation, in structural relationships governing story existents, in point of view, in intertextuality, and in a sense of closure. These indicate a mixture of bottom-up processes (the first two) and top-down processes (the last three). The purposiveness of a text, on the other hand, is much more elusive, but falls generally within the areas of social practice and ideology referred to above.

One further point useful to clarify here is that apparent resemblances between this approach to reading and the implications for reading of the distinction between *langue* and *parole*, which was a central tenet of structuralism, are entirely superficial. This structuralist concept generates the argument that if a particular speech act (*parole*) is a specific realization of the underlying system of language (*langue*), so particular narratives might constitute realizations of a more universal 'deep' narrative structure. This description only applies very narrowly to the difference between top-down and bottom-up reading processes, and in practice has tended to operate in defining particular instances of works which bundle together generically, so that for children's literature 'Romance', 'School Story', 'Fantasy', 'New Realism', and so on, each constitutes a *langue*. Moreover, the analogy needs to be further modified in the light of more recent linguistic theory. Birch (1989) points out that such an opposition valorizes an ideal construct over everyday usage, and Fairclough (1989, p. 22), argues that *langue* is not homogeneous, and that *parole* has to be understood not as an individualistic language use, but as socially determined language use. In other words, we might expect to find some degree of struggle within discourse between an attempt at individual self-expression and the explicit and implicit constraints social structures and ideologies place upon expression. This is especially problematic with literary narrative, which, as a dialogic mode, is on the one hand subject to influence from other kinds of *langue*, and on the other hand may have motives for being which readily cross genre boundaries. It is only fair to add, though, that within late structuralism and recent narratological theory efforts to link readings of narrative texts with analyses of social practices, as evidenced in, say, Roland Barthes' semiotic readings of culture and Mieke Bal's feminist narratological readings of the Bible, have offered various ways to situate theories of narrative within a socio-cultural perspective. While modern narratology owes much to structuralism for its early development, it has long been clear that another kind of linguistics is needed for effective analysis of textuality.

What I have been arguing so far is set out in Figure 1.1, which outlines my proposed distribution of the various components of narrative between story and discourse. The distribution is made on the basis that *story* comprises what we might roughly think of as 'what certain characters do in a certain place at a certain time', and *discourse* comprises the complex process of encoding that story which involves choices of vocabulary, of syntax, of order of presentation, of how the narrating voice is to be orientated towards what is narrated and towards the implied audience, and so on. I am now going to examine how these components function within the text of a picture book, and will use the opening page of Leon Garfield's text of *The Writing on the Wall* (illustrated Michael Bragg, 1983) as my starting point. The story of this book is a retelling of the biblical account of Belshazzar's feast, but refocused as experienced by a palace kitchen boy. It has an overtly articulated moral, but a much more complex significance, involving power, pride, abasement and, very significantly, language and communication:

> Just as Sam is short for Samuel, so Samuel was short for a boy. Very short. When he fetched the dishes in, all you could see was roast goose and legs. When he took the dishes out, all you could see were dirty plates and legs. The most you ever saw of his other end was a tuft of hair sticking up over the top of sprouts or dumplings, like a sprig of black parsley. He was a nothing, a nobody; he was a kitchen-boy in Babylon, and he was rushed off his feet.
>
> (Garfield and Bragg, *The Writing on the Wall*, p. 4)

What story-elements can be deduced from this discourse? While it is only the beginning of a more extended narrative, it quickly imparts and marks as important some features of character, setting and role, and the picture within which the text is visually embedded adds more substance to these. We hear and see that Samuel is a boy, small of size, who works as a kitchen-boy in Babylon; the

STORY (what is narrated)	DISCOURSE (the narrating)
Events: Actions Happenings ⎦ processes (improvements deteriorations) Existents: Characters/Actors Setting ⎾ time ⎿ place	Processes of Selection (what is <u>read</u>, but includes both what is stated and what implied) Mode: narrative descriptive argumentative Narrative Processes: (a) Narrating agent(s): narrator(s) implied author (b) Receptors: narratee(s) implied reader Point of view from which 'story' presented: Narrator p.o.v. character focalization ideology (overt/implicit) Order (or sequence) Duration Relation (connections between 'story' existents) Specifications of setting Symbols, allusions, intertexts

Figure 1.1 Components of story and discourse

actions performed in this stretch of narrative are the carrying of full dishes to the dining tables and the carrying of dirty dishes away.

On the other hand, the narrative is rather elliptical, and leaves a very substantial gap between the second and third sentences. Immediately apparent, then, is the engagement of readers through the pervasive practice of narrative discourse of making only partial representations and requiring audiences to fill gaps and make inferences to supply what is not there. In this particular example, the connection is finally made explicit in the concluding sentence of the paragraph ('he was a kitchen-boy'). The effect here, obviously enough, is very different from beginning the narrative with, say, 'Samuel was a kitchen-boy at the court of Belshazzar, King of Babylon', which would be a more informative opening in terms of *story* components, in that it would economically give the audience information about character and about both the temporal and spatial aspects of setting. In proceeding in this way, however, the narrative would also have a significant discoursal implication, in so far as it indicated the genre as 'Bible story' and might then activate in the audience immediate recourse to the particular top-down cognitive strategies conventionally called upon by this genre (that is, expectations of: examples of exemplary or moral behaviour, or the consequences of its opposite; supernatural or miraculous interventions in the story; traces of a specialized language; etc.). It might also, of course, stimulate immediate resistance from other audience members unsympathetic to the genre. Instead, the opening departs drastically from the conventional, story-focused 'once upon a time' beginning, with its concentration on events and existents. Another way to say this is that there is a discrepancy between discourse-order and story-order. This estranging discrepancy, I suggest, both makes it less likely that ready generic expectations will be called to mind and compels the audience to focus attention on some particular details whose relevance to the story may not be immediately apparent. My argument is that these details give *theme* a status at least equal to the status of story. My discussion has, of course, now shifted to the components of discourse listed above, so let's now examine these more systematically, keeping in mind the questions, 'How does the discourse convey the story elements, and what does it convey about them?'

Discoursal modes

In Figure 1.1, I listed three items under the heading 'Mode'. These represent three distinct discoursal modes (narrative, descriptive and argumentative) which may, nevertheless, co-occur within very short stretches of text. Most recent fiction probably uses the first two principally, and tends only to introduce the argumentative mode – the

most overt agent of ideology in the text – by locating it within conversations carried out between various fictional characters inside
the narrative. Any views thus expressed are not obviously attribut-
able to either narrator or author, though it is often not hard to see
where authorial sympathies lie. The opening paragraph of *The Writing on the Wall* conforms to the expectation that its modes will be
narrative and descriptive, but the opening sentence playfully constructs a logical relationship which parodies the argumentative
mode. The correlatives, 'Just as . . . so', and the repetition of key
words assert the sameness of the linked propositions:

> Just as Sam   is   short for Samuel
>   so Samuel was short for a boy.

But because the shared pivot signifier *short for* points to quite different signifieds ('an abbreviation of' and 'undersized'), the analogy
proves to be both comic and self-deconstructing. Audiences may
not be especially aware of the effect of this game with mode and
meaning, but the effect is to foreground the slipperiness of meaning
and its dependence on context here at the beginning of a narrative
within which the interpretation of signs and the power to control
their significances is a principal theme. This power becomes crucial
for the outcome of Samuel's story when Daniel, 'wisest man of the
Jews', replaces the signifier *wanting* in the message 'You have been
weighed in the balances and found wanting' (from Daniel 5:27)
with a signifier synonymous with one of the signifieds of *wanting*,
that is, *needing*. Through this wordplay, the text then formulates its
concluding, overt message: 'God punishes greed, not need' (articulated, as I suggested above, as the direct speech of an authoritative
character).

Narrative processes

Distinctions which have long been observed in narrative fiction are
those between author, implied author and narrator, and then more
recently, by a symmetrical extension, analysts began using the equivalent differences between the reader, the implied reader and the
narratee (the implied audience for the narrator's discourse; that is,
an audience constructed within or implicit in the text). Any discussion of point of view in literature (whether in poetry or fiction) must
address these distinctions. In verse the constructed speaking voice
is conventionally called the *persona* and in the novel the *narrator*.

Not all theorists recognize three pairs here, and in many narratives there may be no function discernible for, say, the implied author or for the narratee, though if text is to be thought of as a form of inter-personal communication, the presence of one at least implies the presence of its counterpart. My own practice, which I will discuss more fully in Chapter 2, is to consider the Implied Author/Implied Reader pair as a construction within texts which has little, if any, narrative function, but which operates principally as the bearer of implicit social practices and ideological positions.

Such discriminations generate a narrative transaction frame which can be represented as in Figure 1.2. As this figure indicates, the only narrative transactions which can actually be observed within the discourse of a narrative fiction, that is, the speech acts by which information is communicated from a speaker to an audience, occur either as narrator narrating to narratee, or as part of the func-tions performed by characters (which may include intratextual nar-rator or narratee roles within embedded narratives – that is, when a character tells a story). The major function of the narrator/narratee transaction is to mediate the further relationship between writer and reader which, because it exists outside the transactional frame,

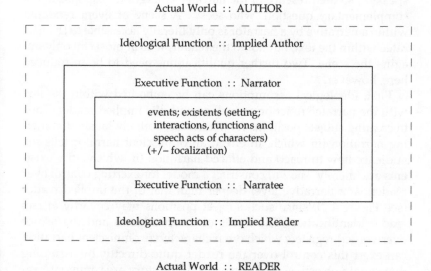

Actual World : : AUTHOR

Ideological Function : : Implied Author

Executive Function : : Narrator

events; existents (setting;
interactions, functions and
speech acts of characters)
(+/– focalization)

Executive Function : : Narratee

Ideological Function : : Implied Reader

Actual World : : READER

Figure 1.2 Frame of narrative transactions

cannot in itself be observed. The distance between narratee and reader can vary, just as can the distance between narrator and author, but because the reader cannot literally enter the fictional world, but encounters at one remove the narration of a narrator to a narratee (or more than one narratee), the gap can never be completely bridged; in fact the narratee like the narrator is an existent within the confines of the narrative transaction. The function is perhaps most evident when the narrator is unreliable, as happens most obviously in first-person narration, because readers will dissociate themselves from a credulous narratee. Narratees are less evident in third-person narrations, which can employ a relatively impersonal narrative mode, and which often assume narrator reliability. Such narratives may imply a narratee point of view, though this probably happens more frequently with picture books than with words-only texts.

As the reference to picture books suggests, the presence of a narratee can be shown even when the narrator is effaced – that is, when the narrator is not rendered as an overtly present subject by the use of such pronominal deictics as 'I' or 'you', or by the use of overtly emotive language within the narrative or descriptive modes. As the presence of the narrator emerges in response to the question 'who speaks?', so the presence of the narratee emerges in response to the complementary question 'who sees?'. A scene or event rendered within a narrative by a narrator is only literally accessible to the narratee within the text, but not to the reader, who at most can only imagine the scene. Two further qualifications need to be introduced here, however.

First, ideological assumptions can be embodied within the text with the narratee function as well as with the implied reader. Thus in creating subject positions for a narratee, both obviously dominating narration (in which, in effect, an omniscient narrator tells the audience how to react) and effaced narration (in which story existents are 'merely' shown) construct a model for exerting control over readers at a narrative level deeper than that of the implied reader (see Figure 1.2), since such subject positions may covertly attract reader identification. The forms of direct address and the use of overworded registers which often characterize omniscient narration can exert this control over the reader quite directly, by assuming that certain objectives and outcomes of the story are commonsensically natural and desirable. We have no doubt that in *The Writing on the Wall* it is fitting that Belshazzar should be punished for his arrogance and presumption and there should be some compensation for Samuel's lowliness.

Effaced narration can be even more powerful in implying that particular assumptions are a matter of common knowledge, shared between narrator and narratee. A good example of such effaced narration is Steven Kellog's *The Island of the Skog* (1973). The story of this book concerns a group of mice who, tiring of persecution by larger animals, decide to emigrate. They sail to an island with one inhabitant (the 'skog') and try to usurp his possession by violence, but all is resolved peacefully. The book begins as follows:

> It was National Rodent Day, and Jenny decided to have a party. Hanna, Wooster, and Louise came. So did Bouncer and his buddies from the bowling alley.
>
> (Kellog, *The Island of the Skog*, p. 5)

There is nothing here which overtly marks the presence of a narrator, except that *somebody* is telling this story, and this somebody uses such colloquial clichés as 'buddies from the bowling alley'. On the whole, the narration at this stage concentrates on the existents of the story that is beginning: time, place, character. The joke in this opening sentence, with its parody of human celebratory days, is not drawn attention to as it is in Garfield's text. The grammatical subject positions in all other clauses are occupied by the characters being introduced. The narrative subsequently admits a few small examples of overt narratorial attitude, but generally the characters are made to disclose theme through their words and actions. Once again, the audience happily accepts the assumption that the story outcome is desirable: aggression is displaced by negotiation and friendliness, and the quest for an aggression-free environment is neatly achieved. Since for most educated people this is a culturally desirable outcome, it is unlikely to be questioned. We might also ask, though, whether we should as readily accept the process by which the quest is achieved, in that its paradigm is in effect a colonialist appropriation of a New World in which an immigrants' utopia is constructed after obtaining the consent and co-operation of the aboriginal inhabitant. (I suspect there is a joke about the American Pilgrim Fathers here.) The issues are sharply focused just after the mice first sight the island:

> 'The book calls it the Island of the Skog,' said Wooster. 'It says: "Population: One Skog." But it doesn't say what a Skog is.'

'If there's only one, then there's plenty of room for all of us,' said
Louise. 'Why don't we bring it a gift so it will know we're friendly?'

'Wait a minute, flubberhead,' snapped Bouncer. 'Suppose this Skog
is dangerous? Let's blaze our way to the island and show him we mean
business!'

(Kellog, *The Island of the Skog*, p. 15)

Wooster's contribution of 'neutral' information is analogous to an
effaced narrator: it is authoritative – 'the book . . . says' – without
disclosing the source of its authority; it specifies an existent, but
withholds further information about it. Historians will notice how
closely the formulation comes to the notion of the *terra nullius*, the
European legal ruling ('the book' now heavily imbued with particular ideology) which was used in the seventeenth and eighteenth
centuries to justify colonization of New World countries such as the
Americas and Australia by declaring them effectively uninhabited.
The two other characters (here Wooster's narratees) draw alternative inferences from this information, namely that friendliness is
called for, and that violence is called for. But the whole exchange is
structured so as to exclude other possibilities, and as such is a construction of narrative which has a potential to be ideologically very
powerful. We might decide that in this case the colonialist paradigm is both deeply buried and ameliorated, since the initial
military invasion is revealed to be destructive and counter-produc-
tive, serving only to alienate the skog and inspire a guerrilla
resistance. It might thus rather seem that, thematically, the outcome
illustrates the necessity for male abruptness and aggression to be
neutralized by female thoughtfulness and gentleness. But in neither
case could it be effectively shown that the ideology implicit in the
colonialist paradigm has been nullified or silenced.

The second qualification to the separation of narratee and reader
mentioned above inheres in the special nature of picture books. The
pictures do offer the reader at least a representation of what is being
described, and in *The Writing on the Wall*, as in good picture books
generally, text and pictures in tandem create significance and point
of view. The audience has no scope to find a dissenting opinion
when, for example, a picture of an overweight Belshazzar eating
strawberries with a ladle appears in conjunction with the overtly attitudinal description, 'he spooned up strawberries as bright as
blood, and poured on cream as thick as pride' (see Plate 1). We also
become aware, I think, that we 'see' the other characters as Samuel

Plate 1 *The Writing on the Wall* (detail)

sees them (obviously so in the strawberries episode, where Samuel is in the lower right-hand corner, seen from behind, and so looking 'into' the scene, with his head forming a continuous line with the bowl of strawberries and the ladle); conversely, however, we don't see Samuel as the other characters in the text might see him, and perhaps the main thematic point emerging here is that they don't see him at all, they only see his function ('Hey there, roast potatoes, or whatever your name is! Over here!'). In so far as the other characters have active roles in the text, and are not just acted upon, they too occupy subject positions, and represent one point of view towards Samuel, which the narratee partly shares ('all *you* could see was'). The *reader* is thus offered a number of possible subject positions from which to view characters and events, and the narrator–narratee relationship constructs at least a double role for the reader: a subject position as one of the feasters, and a subject position which shares the narrator's contempt for the feasters and sympathy for the child.

It is not really possible, though, to share more than a physical point of view with the feasters, because by the second page of text the reader is compelled to share the narrator's view of the feasters. If we are not deterred by their treatment of Samuel, we can hardly resist the attitudinal shaping of their description:

> All the rich and mighty of Babylon had come: dukes and duchesses, generals and admirals, lawyers and bankers and their wives sat cheek by costly cheek, and swigged and guzzled to the greater glory of Belshazzar, the King.
>
> (Garfield and Bragg, *The Writing on the Wall*, p. 7)

Because Samuel's story is added as the frame for the biblical event, because, as in the above list for example, some of the character-functions exist in the modern world, and because of the attitude expressed towards 'the rich and mighty', the book develops as theme a socio-economic stance relevant to the modern world – the abuse of wealth and power, and the indulgence of self while others are in visible need, and perhaps they have greater force than the correspondingly abbreviated biblical story, with its themes of humility and recognition of the Hebrew God. It is thus significant that Samuel finally gets to feed the starving cat, Mordecai, when everybody's attention is distracted by the writing on the wall. Structurally, of course, we are dealing with two interrelated stories which have interrelated themes.

Strategies of narration, then, are central to the question of point of view, the construction of an attitude towards the story events and existents, and I now turn to that issue.

POINT OF VIEW

Point of view is the aspect of narration in which implicit authorial control of audience reading strategies is probably most powerful.

Peter Hunt (1988a) has argued – and he is quite right – that implicit authorial control is a characteristic marker of the discourse of children's fiction. The impulse of readers to surrender themselves to the shaping discourse renders them susceptible to the power in point of view to impose a subject position from which readers will read. For this reason, adults who wish for children to develop unrestricted reading strategies and to be able to identify and resist restrictive texts will need to teach children to recognize how point of view is constructed in discourse.

Point of view may be discussed under two broad headings.

(1) *Perceptual* point of view. If, with reference to the existents represented in a text – its objects, events, people, landscape, etc., we ask the question, 'Who sees?', we are trying to determine the perceptual point of view, the vantage point from which something is represented as being visualized. Such visualization can be an activity of the narrator of the text, or of a character situated within the text. Another way to put this is to say that phenomena are *focalized* by some perceiving agent, whom we can call the focalizer. There can be a lot of switching between narrator focalization and character focalization, and between various characters, though in children's literature it is unusual to find narratives extensively focalized by more than a narrator plus, say, one main character. The point of noticing who is the text's focalizer at any moment is tied up with attitude-making and the credence we give as readers to what the text offers. Often perceptual point of view merges into the second kind of point of view, which I will call *conceptual,* where the answer to the question 'Who sees/perceives?' will include an attitudinal judgement.

(2) *Conceptual* point of view. Conceptual point of view comprises all intratextual acts of interpretation of all kinds. These involve: interpretations made in response to perceptual observations; interpretations made in response to other stimuli, such as events, happenings, or the actions of other characters; interpretations (often implicit ones) based on the ideological stance of the focalizer. These are arrived at slightly differently in novels and picture books, though since the overall effect is the same I shall only illustrate it here with William Mayne's novel *Drift* (1985).

This example quickly demonstrates how point of view can be

marked as focalization by processes of visualization, and then how quickly it moves into a conceptual frame.

> The Indian girl was trying to catch a crow that had stayed in the village by the lake all winter. The girl's name was Tawena, and she lived in the tents and cabins at the end of the village.
> Rafe Considine watched her, sitting on a heap of hard snow outside his own door. Tawena was throwing down balls of suet from a lump of fat she had in her hand. Now and then she ate some herself. She had a fatty face, Rafe thought, and brown eyes deep in the fat. He was sure she had stolen the suet. The tent and cabin people had nothing much to live on, but some of them were well-covered.
>
> (Mayne, *Drift*, p. 7)

There are a number of switches that take place here. The first two sentences are, for lack of any other information, read as *narrator-focalized*. The first describes something that is happening – the attempt of the girl to catch the crow – but also includes information either not pertinent to the present action (the fact that the village is by a lake) or information that cannot be deduced visually (the crow had been in the village all winter). It's also pertinent to note how discourse uses verb tense here to create a spatio-temporal illusion: the past progressive tense, 'the girl *was trying* to catch a crow', quickly creates the impression that 'the past tense indicates the present' (see Martin 1986, p. 137), with the past perfect – 'the crow *had stayed* in the village' – taking over the function of the simple past. The shifting of tense forward in time in this way is very common in narrative discourse, and is also exemplified by selection of indicators of closeness (proximal deictics) – for example, 'this', 'here', 'now' – rather than the corresponding indicators of remoteness (distal deictics) – 'that', 'there', 'then'. The strategy narrows the distance between narrator and characters, as also in effect does the use of the definite article ('*the* village') to refer to an existent which has not been previously specified: the article implies that both sender and receiver in an interpersonal speech act already possess the essential background knowledge. Or, to put it within the narrative transactional frame, the narrator appears to assume that the narratee is familiar with that existent. The structure of the discourse, in both micro- and macro-operations, neatly illustrates how in general assumptions may be inscribed within texts.

The closeness of narrator and narratee contributes to the ease with which, in the third sentence, a new character is introduced and now becomes the focalizer (and remains so for the next ninety pages). The shift is formally marked by 'watched'. This verb belongs to a large lexical set whose node is *perceive*, and which is commonly used as an overt signal of focalization. Soon afterwards, the conceptual terms 'thought' and 'was sure' appear, as the character formulates opinions about what he sees. Finally, the paragraph ends with an unmarked, untagged, utterance which, following so closely after the two conceptual verbs, will be understood as a thought in Rafe's mind: 'The tent and cabin people had nothing much to live on, but some of them were well-covered.' The thought implies an ideological position, an implicitly pejorative comment on a subordinate social group. The hint, difficult to verify, that 'well-covered' is adult language, discloses that the prejudice is socially learned.

Mayne's constructions of point of view are very subtle, and this example is typical of the way he cultivates a fallible character-focalized narration, rather than the narratorial presentation of character-focalization more typical of fiction for children. The effect is doubled in *Drift*, in which the same 'story' is told twice, once by Rafe and once by Tawena, in a very elegant illustration of how deeply a 'story' and its significance are implicated in discourse.

TOP-DOWN AND BOTTOM-UP READING

Earlier in this chapter I referred to the distinction between approaching texts from the macro-discoursal perspective, that is, reading 'top-down', and from the micro-discoursal, or reading 'bottom-up'. I suggested then that a comprehensive reading of narrative discourse would use both kinds of operation. 'Top-down' reading draws on higher order knowledge to help make a text intelligible and so has recourse to world knowledge and prior knowledge of content areas, of genres, of narrative codes, and of conventions which make discourse coherent, such as conversational principles. Bottom-up reading begins with words in small stretches of language, that is with lexis, semantics and syntax, and works upwards from there to 'meaning'. The two interact because while there is always a top-down developmental, experiential and/or cultural factor present, interpretation of a written text must finally rest on its linguistic components. Here I want to illustrate the interaction by trying to talk about some examples in which it seems possible to stress one more than the other.

That the differences between top-down and bottom-up reading are not just an issue of concern to educationists, literary theorists and linguists is evident from children's literature itself, because in some genres the difference is inscribed thematically, frequently as culture conflict: in fantasy, science fiction, and Robinsonnade (see Maher, 1988) for example, it is possible to place characters in situations of extreme cultural difference, in which they interpret situations top-down according to disparate social assumptions. Top-down and bottom-up interpreting are thus brought into conflict. The post-disaster novel offers many examples in which the disclosure of top-down interpretations as partial or erroneous challenges readers to reconsider their own practices of top-down and bottom-up reading. Thus Parts 2 and 3 of Louise Lawrence's widely read *Children of the Dust* (1985) dramatize the mental struggles of young people born and raised in a bunker to grasp an outside world utterly different from their own, and not susceptible to the same cultural interpretations. Caroline Macdonald's *The Lake at the End of the World* (1988) reuses the motif in an overtly dialogic novel, in which 'young man from the bunker' and 'young woman from outside' act as alternating narrators, misinterpreting situations because they share few cultural assumptions. Again, it is the inconsistent relationship between top-down knowledge and bottom-up processing that enables the children in Nicholas Fisk's *Grinny* to deduce that their mysterious visitor is not from Earth.

Such thematic inscription of top-down/bottom-up interaction would make an interesting study in itself. For now I will take a simpler example, a picture book whose conclusion is a stretch of text in which meaning is determined by top-down processes and a complete bottom-up decoding is probably beyond the ability of the expected audience, though that audience is also probably quite satisfied with the general sense arrived at. Intelligibility is partly facilitated by an effect whereby previously acquired knowledge enables the decoding of quite complex lexical structures. The book, Garfield and Bragg's *King Nimrod's Tower* (1982), is an (earlier) companion piece to *The Writing on the Wall*, and uses the same refocusing of a known story through an apparently unimportant character and also expresses a metalinguistic interest in language and communication. In this book, Garfield's text frames a retelling of the story of the Tower of Babel with a story about a boy's attempts to compel a stray dog to behave so that he can take it home. God, who (as ultimate top-down interpreter) watches both stories, is more interested in the boy and the dog than in King Nimrod, though his only intervention is to thwart Nimrod's ambition. Directly after the builders are visited with the confusion of tongues, the book ends with this scene:

> 'Sit!' said the boy to his dog. 'I only want to be your friend.'
> And the dog sat.
> 'Stand up!' said the boy to his dog. 'I only want to take you home.'
> And the dog stood up.
> 'Good!' said the boy. 'Now I can take you back to Babylon, and you can sleep beside my bed!'
> So they went.
> 'How did it happen?' marvelled the angels. 'At last!'
> 'Because My Kingdom of Heaven is better reached,' said God, 'by a bridge than by a tower.'
>
> (Garfield and Bragg, *King Nimrod's Tower*, p. 32)

Garfield's decision to conclude his narrative with an aphoristic metaphor is a daring move, since the book's young audience is likely to find the figurative meaning difficult to access by bottom-up decoding. As Winner *et al.* (1979) have suggested, children tend to fail to perceive abstract relationships between physical and psychological properties when encoded in linguistic form. Thus, even if the audience of *King Nimrod's Tower* was developmentally capable of interpreting such a metaphor and of understanding how it valorizes negotiation over aggression in interpersonal relationships, the presence of bridge-like monumental arches in two of Bragg's illustrations of the tower is apt to decompose the bridge–tower opposition. At the worst, though, because at 'story' level the conflict between the boy and dog is brought to such a strong and positive conclusion, the need to shift to the level of thematic significance is not compelling, and so the final utterance may seem merely an appended gnomic mystery of little or no importance. For a slightly more sophisticated reader, whose prior experience of books has generated an expectation that a book is often about more than its story, the metaphor can be more accessible, and is made so by the interaction between top-down and bottom-up processes.

The relevant top-down processes involve prior knowledge about how texts are structured and of what kinds of content might be expected. Thus the audience will infer from the boy's recurrent use of the formula '[X will happen] before I can take you back to Babylon, to sleep beside my bed' that eventually the dog will be taken back to Babylon. This inference makes the story-outcome easy to absorb, and facilitates shifting to another and higher level of interpretation. Secondly, audiences learn a 'grammar' by which simple stories are structured and made internally coherent by cause–effect relationships. The second half of such a grammar as expounded by Stein and Trabasso (1982) moves through three stages highly pertinent to *King Nimrod's Tower*, although it appears here in quite a complex form because the proposed structure is realized simultaneously, but contrapuntally, by the two stories:

ATTEMPT	An overt action or series of actions, carried out in the service of attaining a goal. (Nimrod attempts to build a tower 'as high as heaven'; the boy harangues the dog in order to tame it.)
Cause or Enable	
CONSEQUENCE	An event, action, or endstate, marking the attainment or non-attainment of the protagonist's goal. (The confusion of tongues prevents the building of the tower; the dog goes home with the boy.)
Cause	
REACTION	An internal response expressing the protagonist's feelings about the outcome of his actions, or the occurrence of broader, general consequences resulting from the goal attainment or non-attainment of the protagonist. (The Kingdom is not reached by 'a tower'; the Kingdom is reached by 'a bridge'.)

The top-down interpretative expectations about content and structure are then reinforced by the immediate linguistic structures of the close. The interaction between boy and dog is presented through a transformation of the formulas of command which the boy has regularly uttered, sometimes with accompanying threats (for example, 'Stay or I'll stop your dinner'). Now, by modifying the commands with formulas of friendship, followed by the dog's positive response, and by giving two examples to produce the boy's desired goal, Garfield creates the best possible situation to enable the reader to move from story to theme, from *what* happened to *why* and *how* it happened, and hence he creates the possibility that the reader might also draw the inference that the concluding metaphor is to be decoded as a concrete thematic statement. Finally, the operation in which top-down processes inform bottom-up decoding adds to the reader's store of knowledge by confirming and reinforcing the expectation that narrative texts do progress from story to thematic significance.

There is a more obvious frame for top-down reading in *King Nimrod's Tower*, of course, and that is a previous familiarity with the biblical story itself, so that the discourse processes and modifications to the existents of that story become foregrounded and audiences may be enabled to grasp from quite early in the text that in part the story is being developed with a thematic and metalinguistic interest in language and communication.

TOP-DOWN, BOTTOM-UP, AND THE REPRESENTATION OF SPEECH

The representation of speech in fiction, and especially of direct speech, is an aspect of narrative discourse to which readers probably apply bottom-up processes rather than top-down, and therefore, for the purposes of my present discussion, illustrates the other end of the spectrum. Conventionally, reader access to characters in conversation is considered to be less mediated than the presentation of those characters in the narrative or descriptive modes, so inferences about thematic significances have to be constructed bottom-up. Although the narrator and the narratee are moved to backgrounded positions for the duration of the conversation, a varying degree of presence may still be indicated by marked *inquit*-tags (that is, the devices for identifying speakers), and these form a further part of the bottom-up decoding. There are some common neutral tags, especially 'said' and 'asked', but almost all tags which convey expressiveness also convey attitude: compare 'he said' with 'he asserted', and 'she asked' with 'she demanded'. My discussion of *The Island of the Skog* earlier showed how the structure of an exchange contributed to a restriction on reader inferencing, and it might be noted how the *inquit*-tagging of the three speakers almost covertly underscored the attitudes: the tags are, 'said Wooster', 'said Louise' and 'snapped Bouncer'. In *The Island of the Skog*, attitude towards story existents (especially character and situation) is consistently to be inferred from quite heavily loaded *inquit*-tags. A complete list for the first ten pages is: announced, puffed, said, cried, cried, declared, cried, insisted, moaned, cried. In this list, the neutral tag 'said' appears only once, so that attitudes towards speech acts are almost constantly being indicated, and become an important part of the data a reader must process to make the text intelligible. A book such as Wagner and Fisher's *The Machine at the Heart of the World* (1983), which demands more top-down processing, makes an interesting comparison, in that there is only one speech utterance tagged with anything other than 'said' (on p. 22 Theobald 'yelled'). Where other, or mixed, modes of speech representation are employed, the narrator is present more overtly. To examine these modes would require another chapter in itself, but would anyway repeat much of what is conveniently available in the taxonomies of Leech and Short (1981, Chapters 9–10) and of Brown (1990).

Examination of *inquit*-tags focuses on the narrative framing of conversation. Texts also encourage inferencing and disclose significance through features of conversational *exchange*. Especially important in guiding reader response are representations of the ways in which power operates in unequal exchanges, and the observation of or control over the principle of turn-taking within an exchange. The application of the principles of pragmatics to the way in which interrelationships are represented in fiction, especially with regard to operations of power in unequal relationships, and to the representations of turn-taking, throws a whole new light on the ways in which texts determine the manner of their own reading. In narrative fiction such conversational exchanges are normally represented in conjunction with more obvious modes of narrator intervention. In the following example Shofiq is attempting to get some information on behalf of his father from an employee of the Social Security department. A narrative commentary is built into the scene by including the reactions of Shofiq's friend Bernard. Shofiq lacks power in the exchange for three different reasons, so stands little chance of success: he is 'the public', lacking certain information, confronted with officialdom; he is a child; and he is an English 'Pakistani'. He expresses his enquiry fully and clearly, and the scene then continues:

> The girl actually smiled. Not a very friendly smile, but she smiled.
> 'Very good' she said. 'I can tell you it's a real relief to find one of you lot that can speak the language! I suppose you were born here?'
> 'Yes, miss,' replied Shofiq.
> 'Live down the Brook?'
> 'Yes, miss.'
> She made a 'humph' sound in her throat and pulled a pad of paper towards her.
> 'Right? What was all that again?'
> Shofiq didn't bat an eyelid. Bernard was already beginning to smart. She was so *rude*. She was so ruddy rude. He swallowed noisily. Shofiq looked at him and scowled, warningly, as if to say 'Keep your mouth shut!'
> The girl said: 'If you're going to make funny faces all day, kindly do it elsewhere. I'm very busy.'
> 'I'm sorry, miss,' said Shofiq. 'What I wanted to know was . . .'
> The girl made squiggles on the paper while he went through it all again, and a lot more. She didn't make proper notes though, because Bernard watched her. When Shofiq had finished she smiled.
> 'Well, that's that then,' she said. 'I can't help you, I'm afraid.'
> (Jan Needle, *My Mate Shofiq*, p. 116)

Shofiq remains calm and polite, employing the honorific address 'miss' and apologizing when accused of misbehaviour, but because he is the one in the supplicant role he is unable to take charge of the direction of the exchange. Thus the woman ignores all he says prior to this part of the exchange and immediately shifts attention to discourse rather than its import, and reinforces her rudeness semantically ('one of you lot'). She further controls the exchange by pursuing her remark with requests for irrelevant information which she then implies is to Shofiq's detriment. Bernard's identification of the rudeness underlying her speech overtly articulates how the exchange is being structured, and becomes a focus for the rudeness to irrupt openly. The assertion 'I'm very busy' merely reiterates her possession of power – she is, after all, making Shofiq needlessly repeat his story. Much of the analysis of class and race prejudice in *My Mate Shofiq* is expressed through such representations of conversation.

The Social Security officer's rudeness is identifiable, then, largely because of hiatuses in the sequencing of the exchange. An important top-down element in the comprehension of conversation as connected and coherent discourse was identifed by H.P. Grice (1975). Grice suggested that conversation is informed by a group of unstated rules with which speakers co-operate for mutual benefit. He termed this process the *co-operative principle*, and preferred to call the 'rules' *maxims*, since, though they clearly exist, they may readily be broken. He proposed four conversational maxims. The first of these is *quantity*, whereby the response to a preceding utterance is just the amount required, neither more nor less; this maxim is broken all the time in ordinary conversation, and often also in literary writing. The second maxim is that of *quality*, which points to the truthfulness of the reply, and is breached when the second speaker tells lies, or fictionalizes. The third maxim is that of *relation*, and demands relevance, and so an irrelevant change of subject, as with the Social Security officer's questions, breaches this maxim. It may seem to be closely related to the more linguistically defined concept of cohesion, but where cohesion is dependent upon the linguistic signifiers chosen, and their relationship, the maxim of relation points to the signifieds and their relationship. The fourth maxim is that of *manner*; this is the least clearly defined of the four, but its general import is that the reply should be orderly and unambiguous, in a similar register, and framed lucidly. Whenever one of these maxims is violated, the ellipses or gaps left between the two speakers produce sub-textual meanings, which Grice termed *implicatures*. Since these maxims suggest a norm, and are in fact often violated, the ways in which they are utilized or breached become a key aspect of signification, and enable an audience to make interpretative or evaluative judgments about what is represented in the text.

The maxims are a group of loosely constituted pragmatic principles which a speaker assumes are shared by his/her addressee(s). Their essence lies more in common sense than in linguistically describable features of text, and involve a large degree of subjectivity in their application. It is, of course, impossible to determine finally what is 'too much' for quantity, or where the parameters of 'truthfulness' lie, but the work of Sperber and Wilson (1986) on relevance and on assumptions shared (to varying extents) by speakers in mutual cognitive environments proves very helpful in elucidating this area of human communication. Conversation in fiction is always a constructed artifice, not the more spontaneous phenomenon of everyday speech acts, and in this specialized context the subjective element in the application of conversational maxims may tempt readers to over-infer psychological motivation in fictional situations, or to under-emphasize aspects of text which may be of greater significance in specific situations, but the maxims are, nevertheless, useful pointers to features which need to be included within analyses of continuous stretches of discourse which comprise or include dialogue. Studies in pragmatics have subsequently refined and extended Grice's thoughts, notably by the identification of the 'Politeness Principle' in conversation whereby social conventions of tact, generosity, modesty or praise over-ride simple applications of cooperative principles (see Leech 1983, pp. 104–49).

BOTTOM-UP DECODING AS A CONFIRMATION OF TOP-DOWN ASSUMPTIONS

The representation of conversational exchange does require audiences to call on their world knowledge to achieve the fullest comprehension, but sometimes the effect of piecing together the bits of the discourse is to construct an affirmation of some societal assumption. Consider Plate 2, from a 'supermarket' picture book, *A New Coat for Spikey*. The text goes:

Spikey hated his prickles.
"I don't like my new coat," he wailed.
"It's ugly. I look like a cactus."

"You'll learn to like it, Spikey," said his father.
"It's the right coat for you."

Plate 2 *A New Coat For Spikey*

> Spikey hated his prickles.
> 'I don't like my new coat,' he wailed.
> 'It's ugly. I look like a cactus.'
> 'You'll learn to like it, Spikey,' said his father.
> 'It's the right coat for you.'
>
> (Redhead and Dickinson, *A New Coat for Spikey*, pp. 6–7)

Here, in quite obvious ways, text and picture interrelate by functioning as mutual glosses. The text contains semantically full words like *hated*, *wailed* and *ugly*, and a dialogue between parent and child, though none of these features is actually represented in the picture, apart from a link between 'wailed' and the tears falling from Spikey's right eye. Instead, the picture reinforces the parental message, as the arm around the child on the right-hand page reinforces the words:

> 'You'll learn to like it, Spikey,' said his father.
> 'It's the right coat for you.'

This advice is also the only speech in this twenty-four-page book not spoken by the main character, and so comes with all the weight of paternalistic parental authority. More obliquely, the happy playing of Spikey's sisters (left-hand page) counterpoints Spikey's expression of discontent, and combines with the audience's extra-textual knowledge that hedgehogs are supposed to have prickles to define Spikey's attitude as misguided. The object of this book is to inculcate contentment with one's own state and appearance, a message which is thus foreshadowed at the very moment in the book when the wrong-thinking character first gives expression to his discontent with the way things are.

The dialogue between the two characters here also exemplifies another aspect of the way the dynamics of exchange function to present pivotal power or authority elements within relationships. It is an aspect of books for young children that they use a small vocabulary and much repetition, which can have the effect of producing a highly cohesive text. Such cohesive repetition is, of course, also desirable in narratives for young audiences who have not yet developed a strong sense of connectedness in narrative (see Toolan 1988, pp. 193–202). Clearly, a series of utterances which are linked by strong cohesion but which also contain new actions or ideas build on whatever grasp of narrativity an audience may have, and

may even help to foster a developing sense of narrative, of related-
ness of utterances and events, and of cause-and-effect relationships.
At the same time, though, cohesion can demand particular attitudinal responses and can establish, or perhaps enforce, particular
power relationships. If the language in the above exchange is categorized as 'pejorative', 'neutral' and 'positive', it is readily seen that
of the semantic items, all those expressing Spikey's feelings are pejorative, apart from 'coat', whereas his father's are neutral to positive:

Pejorative	Neutral	Positive
hated		
don't like		will learn to like
wailed	said	
prickles	new coat	the right coat
ugly		
like a cactus		

The young hedgehog rejects the self he is becoming, and the use of
the simple simile, 'I look like a cactus', is a simple example of how
the self may be defined as if it were some undesirable other. The
parent, represented as expressing positive attitudes through his
moderate language and capable of a perspective on the future, is
able to affirm and quietly assert the rightness of Spikey's selfhood.

There are, then, several communicative functions performed simultaneously by this discourse stretch (a discourse which, because of
these multiple functions, turns out to be much more complex than a
casual glance would suggest, and certainly far more complex than
its target audience could possibly begin to realize). An important
thing about these functions is their inextricability. At the same time
as it reinforces the audience's ability to descry connectedness the
text exploits that very connectedness to affirm a major tenet of our
culture (that individuals should learn to be content with the un-
changeable elements of their own selfhood). Whether or not this
particular tenet is 'good' in a philosophical or ethical sense is not
my immediate concern here: what is, is the power to acculturate the
audience which inheres in such a textual situation.

Formal cohesive links are powerful in the way just described, but
the overall coherence of a stretch of discourse also depends on the
capacity of the text to communicate its functions. A major element

in the creation of comic effects is the absence of fit between the capacity of cohesive devices to assert the connectedness of an utterance and the semantic components of the utterance itself. Such effects are already to be found in picture books, and are prominent in books written for readers just moving into more substantial stretches of text. They are especially important in comic writing, as illustrated by the following extract from Diana Wynne Jones' *The Four Grannies* (1980). There are four components to the exchange, which I have numbered:

> [Erg has just presented his grannies with a heap of washing to distract their attention from his own doings.]

> [1]   Granny Two sprang up saying she would fill the sink with nice hot water.

> [2]   'You're allowed to use the washing machine,' Erg said.

> [3]   'Oh no, dear,' said Granny Two. 'Electricity doesn't mix with water. It gets into the clothes, you know.'

> [4]   On reflection, Erg thought that washing in the sink would keep them busier.

> (Wynne Jones, *The Four Grannies*, p. 50)

The four stages of this exchange reflect and parody a four-step reasoned argument. Step 1 represents an initial, positively framed proposition, and while it is encoded as indirect speech, the phrase 'nice hot water' clearly represents speech characteristic of a particular speaker. Step 2 represents a counter-proposition, combining a concessive permission ('allowed') with a technological advantage; there is a strong cohesive link through the semantic contrast of 'sink' and 'washing machine', but also through the absent referent of each utterance, the clothes to be washed. The exchange has thus been shaped inevitably to elicit a cohesive response at Step 3, which must accept or refuse the alternative offered and hence the permission.

So far, then, Granny Two's refusal in the first part of 3 is consistent with expectation. But her reason for refusal – while it is semantically cohesive ('electricity . . . water . . . clothes' refer back to 1 and 2), and depends on an utterance which is in isolation experientally correct ('Electricity doesn't mix with water') – is of course nonsense in terms of the reader's own world knowledge and within the immediate wider context, as the further explanation in 3 – 'It gets into the clothes' – makes clear. Formally, without a context, a sentence can have an inherent meaning, but within a context its meaning may change, or become multiple, or, as in this case, virtually disappear. And even as the concluding tag, 'you know', asserts the truth claim of the utterance, it flatters the reader's clear awareness of a different, more solid knowledge. Finally, Step 4 represents the stage in the argument at which the second speaker accedes to the first speaker's position, perhaps on the grounds of its correctness. Here Erg does so, in the form of an unverbalized thought which is again semantically cohesive with the preceding stages of the exchange ('washing in the sink'), but is only coherent within the frame of Erg's private purpose. It might be noted how important different modes of speech and thought representation are in achieving the effects of this exchange. Shifting among ways of representing speech and thought is an important aspect of written language, especially in fiction, and I will return to discuss it in more detail later in this book.

The comic effect, then, is produced not merely because the exchange pivots at Step 3 on assertions that render absurd the referential function of language, but predominantly because the bottom-up structure of the discourse, its connectedness as a cohesive string and process of argument, foregrounds the absurdity particularly sharply.

CLOSURE AND SIGNIFICANCE

How a narrative resolves, 'ties up' or 'untangles' (both metaphors are widespread), the complications of story is a recurrent concern amongst theorists, but is of special interest with children's fiction. Here, the desire for *closure*, both in the specific sense of an achieved satisfying ending and in the more general sense of a final order and coherent significance, is characteristically a desire for fixed meanings, and is apparent in the socializing, didactic purposes of much children's literature. There is an idea that young children require (that is, both 'demand' and 'need') certainties about life rather than indeterminacies or uncertainties or unfixed boundaries. Even a genre such as fantasy, which might be expected to offer a site for a play of meanings and for resistances to fixed meanings, usually shows a strong impulse towards closure. Determinate closures are resisted at times in the works of, in particular, Alan Garner, John Gordon, Tanith Lee and William Mayne, but not in Lloyd Alexander, Susan Cooper, Louise Lawrence or Diana Wynne Jones.

As readers, we learn to look for *some* sense of completeness, both aesthetic and thematic, over and above the bringing of a series of events to a close. Aesthetic completeness is achieved in children's literature through representation of symmetries or movements from states of lack to states of plenitude, as found in, for example: the completion of a quest or purging of an evil; the finding or recovery of a valuable object (Susan Cooper's *Greenwitch*; Leon Garfield's *The Strange Affair of Adelaide Harris*); a return to a place of departure (*Drift*; Gene Kemp's *Jason Bodger and the Priory Ghost*); the replaying of a crucial event, such as the duels in Victor Kelleher's *The Makers*; and so on. The degree of openness in the ending depends on the nature and extent of the instabilities represented in the text and on the extent to which they are resolved, but readers may nevertheless impose closure. John Gordon's *The House on the Brink* has a clear and positive 'story' closure, with the destruction of a physical threat, but remains psychologically and thematically indeterminate. When a colleague asked a class of fourteen-year-olds to read this book, however, she found that without exception they interpreted the book as closed off: for them, the story closure was so significant that it effaced the thematic irresolution. The group had not developed reading strategies which would enable a double reading of such an ending. Finally, a different kind of problem with closure is posed by Ursula Le Guin's *Tehanu*, in which the main strands of story are tied off by the direct intervention of an almost supernatural being (a dragon). This *deus ex machina* ending is so pat that readers are almost compelled to fix attention on the thematic significance – that is, that as Tenar's adopted child Therru/Tehanu discovers her innate and essential subjectivity that enables her to summon the dragon, she also discloses that in the new world coming into being the source of greatest power will now be a woman.

Intentionality can only be fully attributed to a text from the perspective of the close, so a question readers pose retrospectively from the point of view of the ending, is whether the narrative discourse has constructed and ordered the existents of the story in order to produce that particular end (meaning both 'conclusion' and 'significance'). Frank Kermode, writing in *The Sense of an Ending* (1967) of how the representation of time in fiction has most often replicated an apocalyptic sense of time, observes that a common expectation of narrative is that it should be a wholly concordant structure, whose end is in harmony with its beginning, and the middle with both. The end resumes the whole structure. Such a sense of structure is itself an ideological assumption, and it is everywhere informed by what are held to be common cultural assumptions and values. Endings reaffirm what society regards as important issues and preferred outcomes. This still happens even when, as in Cormier's novels, 'good' fails to win out, simply because readers formulate their sense of the ending in those terms. The use of epilogues to mark formal closure has a similar ideological implication: by shifting out of the story-time of the narrative, an epilogue implies a connection with the real time of history (Martin 1986, p. 84) and hence implicitly validates the assumptions of the close. Children's writers do often attempt to resist these pressures in the ending: Kelleher's *The Makers* uses an epilogue, but includes in it many features which indicate that the 'story' is not finally resolved; Mayne in *Salt River Times* and Garfield in *The Prisoners of September* end by shifting attention to marginal and trivial actions.

CONCLUSION

Fiction presents a special context for the operation of ideologies, because narrative texts are highly organized and structured discourses whose conventions may either be used to express deliberate advocacy of social practices or may encode social practices implicitly. They may do both, as when a desired ideological significance is grounded in specific social practices at story level. A text may overtly advocate one ideology while implicitly inscribing one or more other ideologies. Hence the interpretation of such texts will need to take the following factors into account.

The discourse of narratives must be read simultaneously as a linguistic and a narratological process. This includes reference to important discoursal components such as (among others) mode, point of view, narrating voice and order of events. It also includes a compulsion to read narrative discourse both for its story and its significance; ideology operates at both levels.

Significance is constructed by the application of both top-down and bottom-up reading processes, some which readers bring to a text, and some which the structures of the text demand. On the one hand, audiences bring prior knowledge and preconceptions about books and the world to a reading, have assumptions about how narratives are shaped and become meaningful, and bring information from other texts to bear on the text under consideration. On the other hand, textual structures such as the representations of direct speech, and especially conversation, have a powerful influence in implicitly predetermining the significances readers may find. The argumentative discoursal mode may be embedded as a function of character speech which represents advocated values as wise and normal or socially powerful.

Narrative structure, and especially closure, is an ideologically powerful component of texts, since aesthetic completeness and the sense of an appropriate story ending spill over into affirmations of the discourse's thematic conclusions. But an open ending can still be ideologically powerful by evoking particular values and assumptions by its very evasion of them.

Finally, narrative discourse implicitly offers its audiences a range of possible subject positions: aligned with narrators and/or focalizers; in opposition to unreliable narrators or unlikable characters; and so on. The nature of these subject positions is the concern of Chapter 2.

TAKING IT FURTHER

I have argued that within a literary text, relations of power and domination exist in two ways conceptually and in two main ways narratively. Conceptually, there is the dilemma for both writers and readers that on the one hand ideological practices may be more or less directly advocated while on the other hand ideological assumptions (not necessarily the same ones) will always pervade discourse because they are always implicit within discourse itself. Narratively, these relations exist separately on the planes of 'story' (what is represented) and discourse (the process of representing): that is, characters within the text are represented as affected by the operations of power, and the various mediations between writers and readers are also a form of power relations. A fictional narrative's 'meaning', in its broadest sense, will incorporate all four possibilities, and this principle will apply to any fiction.

A productive way to examine this matrix is to set up comparisons between texts which differ in one or more aspects. The distinction between first-person narration, single-character focalization, and multiple focalization is usually an important beginning point. Compare, for example, Milne's *Winnie the Pooh* with Hoban's *The Mouse and His Child*: to what extent is the representation of idyllic pastoral and anti-pastoral, respectively, affected by the different narrative modes? *Winnie the Pooh* is framed by a first-person narration addressed to an implied reader, but soon switches to address a narratee different from the implied reader; *The Mouse and His Child* is a third-person narration with access to the mental processes of all characters. Again, the quest in Hoban's fiction is for some basic mid-twentieth-century Western values – home, family and open community, and 'self-winding' (that is, the independence of the individual) – and this tends to mean that there is not a large gap between explicit and implicit ideology. This contrasts with the Milne, where the implicit underpinning ideological practices of a culture and a social class are, critically speaking, the important areas of ideology to investigate. Further consideration may be given to the way each book deals with the relationship between concepts and reality, or between private understanding and historical process, and here further comparison might be made with Peter Dickinson's *A Box of Nothing* (1985), in which James, the protagonist and only focalizer, engages on a heroic struggle with being, nothingness and meaning. In general, the effect of focalization on possible reading strategies needs to be considered in any work of fiction.

The narrative representations of ideology and power can also be explored in texts which exist in explicit dialogue with other texts, especially re-versions and sequels. The dialogic effect throws the ideology of both texts into sharp relief. A good example is Robert Leeson's *Silver's Revenge* (1978), a sequel to *Treasure Island* which replicates the narration/focalization by a young member of the group involved. Leeson's recurrent concern with matters of class and race is less overt than in, say, his *The Third Class Genie* (1975), in which the text's significance lies in the resolution of inter-racial conflict, but the concern with these matters still pervades *Silver's Revenge*. This type of intertextual effect will be the subject of Chapter 3.

FURTHER READING

For studies in discourse analysis, see Brown (1990), Cook (1989) and Stubbs (1983). For a substantial introduction to pragmatics see Leech (1983); studies which apply pragmalinguistic principles to literary texts appear from time to time in the *Journal of Pragmatics*. The best study of conversation in fiction is still Leech and Short (1981).

Major studies in theories of narrative and their application are Bal (1985), Chatman (1978), Martin (1986), Rimmon-Kenan (1983) and Toolan (1988). The discoursal construction of dominating narrators has been commented on by Chambers (1977) and Hunt (1988a).

For the interrelationship of discourse, ideology and socialization, see Applebee (1978), Burniston and Weedon (1977) and Hunt (1988a).

TWO

Readers and subject positions in children's fiction

> None of us lives without a reference to an imaginary singularity which we call our 'self'.
>
> (Paul Smith, *Discerning the Subject*, p. 6)

It is not my aim here or elsewhere in this book to engage in a discussion of theories about the crucial concept of the 'subject'. Instead, I will assume a position that has been extensively articulated and defended by others, and attempt to explore its implications for works of children's fiction and the readers of these fictions. I will assume, then, that the subject exists as an individual, but that existence is within a dialectical relationship with sociality. The subject has a singular existence in its self-picturations and the stories it can tell about itself, but these self-constituting moments are just that – *moments* of interpretation within the social relations which produce the subject and which the subject helps to produce (see Paul Smith 1988, especially Chapters 1 and 5; John Smith 1989, pp. 83–5). I think it follows from this assumption that the relationship between a subject's activities as a reader and a work of fiction which is the object of the reading both replicates other forms of subject/sociality interactions and constructs a specular, or mirroring, form of those interactions. On the one hand, the relationship between a reader and a text is dialectical, a negotiation of meaning between a subject's multi-faceted sense of self and the many interpretative positions which a text may make possible. On the other hand, a work of fiction itself to some degree always mirrors the kinds of picturation and narrative which the subject draws upon for its own sense of selfhood, and it especially replicates the pragmatic functions of language in the actual world through which interpersonal relationships are constituted. The subject as reader is thus confronted with numerous examples in which the subjectivity of a fictive character is constructed and defined not merely in terms of

47

its own being, as incorporated by the character's represented actions, speech and thought processes, but also as it is narrated and described, and as it is perceived by other characters and interacts with them.

Just as I find it necessary to maintain that an individual core of being mediates the subject's experiences of sociality, so also I think it necessary to argue that narrative fictions have referential meaning and are constructed with the intent of shaping reader responses, and hence reader attitudes. This position is often questioned on various grounds: by critics who are inclined to locate meaning only in the reader's response; by Derridean critics, who deny that texts have centres of meaning; and by some materialist 'critical linguists', who locate meaning 'within the context and situation of the text and the institutions that determined its production and reception' (Birch 1989, p. 86). A continuing problem at the heart of the debate is that we can never really know what happens when a reader reads, and this is exacerbated when the reader is a child (and even a listener for whom the text is mediated through adult performance of it). I am nevertheless, as I have done previously (Stephens and Waterhouse 1990), going to insist on the existence of some element of determinable meaning.

As I argued in Chapter 1, a text consists of three interlocked components: the discourse; a 'story' which is ascertained by an act of primary reading (reading for 'the sense'); and a significance, derived by secondary reading from the first two. The implications for subjectivity and for ideology inhere principally at the level of significance, as readers move beyond the primary stage of specular recognition of 'story' to the deeper mirrorings of meaning. Here, the reading subject, as in an actual world pragmatic exchange, may negotiate meaning with the text or be subjected by it. To illustrate this, I will examine two examples of fictive situations in which characters are represented as reading. The first example is a scene early in Libby Hathorn's 'problem' novel/teen-romance *Thunderwith* (1989), in which the main character, Lara, masters literacy through a kind of family-oriented, wide reading programme. Readers will accept this as a positive achievement, because our society on the whole has an ideological commitment to literacy, but as Hathorn represents the process, Lara really only masters 'reading for the sense'. The further significances of the episode are to be deduced by the reader outside the text – a growth in Lara's self-concept and an enrichment of the relationship between mother and daughter. What these books *represent* thematically in the book that in turn alludes to them, then, is more important than what they are. But the significances within the adduced books themselves, however, seem to me to be an interesting and important elision from the text. Here is part of the readings:

> And a world . . . that neither of them had ever dreamed of, opened up for them. They travelled through forests and mountains, in cities of the past and future, to civilisations beyond Earth. They'd found places with the weirdest of names ('Listen to this one, Lara: *Loth- lor-ien*. I can hardly pronounce it but it's so, so beautiful this place, I think we should visit, don't you? After tea?') And they'd wandered through them together. Lara even dreamed about them sometimes.
>
> And as heroes sought rings or maps or treasures and dealt with triumphs or sudden mishaps, Lara and her Mum had laughed and cried together. And they'd talked about the stories when they finished reading. Talked and talked, the way they used to talk about the TV shows they no longer had time to watch.
>
> (Hathorn, *Thunderwith*, p. 6)

The text certainly represents a stimulus to the imagination, but in general the books read are characterized by settings and events (that is, by the existents of 'story'), and reading is a surrender of self to text: in a series of verbs which portray reading as idle engagement, self-introspection, or simple response, the readers here 'visit', 'wander through', 'dream about', 'laugh' and 'cry'. Yet readers of *Thunderwith*, I assume, are expected to extrapolate from this story about story-reading to its unarticulated significance, enacting a turn not taken by the readers *in* the text. Authors whose books are referred to are J.R.R. Tolkien (here) and Susan Cooper. Now, the books of Tolkien and Cooper are profoundly ideological in their purposes, and reading beyond the primary 'sense' ought to lead to recognition of this. What, for example, should a reader make of a book which implies that the best way to think about the world is to do so from the perspective of a conservative upper-middle class English male?

My second example interrogates the process of reading as represented in *Thunderwith*. It occurs towards the end of Caroline Macdonald's post-disaster novel, *The Lake at the End of the World* (1988). In this scene, Hector, a young man born and raised in an underground bunker, which is a totalitarian society where, for example, children and parents are separated, returns to the library to look at the books of his childhood; from a perspective mentally enlarged by a time spent in the outside world, he is able to see how these books fitted in with the community plan for socializing its children. He describes the books, considers the library collection, and concludes: 'There are no other books [in the library] than books like these. So this was my childhood. The world is carefully filtered so I'd know of no other but this' (p. 159). That is, having been exposed to another society outside the bunker, Hector has been empowered to reread the texts of his society in such a way as to see their ideological assumptions. What he has found is that if you read a book and discover that it is utterly free of ideological presuppositions, what that really means is that you have just read a book which precisely reflects those societal presuppositions which you yourself have learned to subscribe to, and which are therefore invisible. Macdonald thus represents a transition from a reader subject position which is one of utter subjection by the text to a dialectical position from which the reader learns about his own subjectivity and the nature of its social relations, and about the society which produced his earlier subjectivity.

Thunderwith and *The Lake at the End of the World* thus both illustrate two ways in which subjectivity is produced in a text, and two different interpretative positions which readers may take up as reading subjects – the subjected and the interrogative. The concept that a fictive text might offer its readers a variety of possible interpretative subject positions is of inestimable importance for reading fiction, and especially for examining the possibility of ideological impact on readers. The subject positions available to children as users of books are often restricted and restrictive, and this is nowhere so sharply defined as by the tendency for these positions to express the ideological assumptions of a society's dominant cultural groups. A function of many books, and sometimes their primary function, is an attempt to change those assumptions.

MULTICULTURALISM AND SUBJECTIVITY IN BOOKS FOR YOUNG READERS

Since the 1960s, in particular, many efforts have been made in both Britain and the USA to produce children's books which critically address tendencies to assume that the world is white, male and middle class. Most notably, in the USA the Council on Interracial Books for Children has sustained a constructive and analytical advocacy since 1965, and in Britain the end of the 1960s saw, for example, the creation of alternative early readers such as the Nippers series. Although this series is now defunct, along with the Reading Schemes the books were designed to redirect into expressing a more open society, the principles are continued in many contemporary picture books. The objectives of such programmes can be defined relatively easily, but the actual implementation faces continuing difficulties, especially since publishers of children's literature favour mass-market books and tend to regard both intercultural and minority culture books as unprofitable and are consequently reluctant either to print them or to maintain them in print. Thus as a proportion of the USA market, books on African American themes have been decreasing since the early 1970s (Greenfield 1986; St Clair 1988); in Australia, where multiculturalism was hardly a concern in children's literature until the 1970s, publishers still rarely commission books from other than Anglo-Celtic authors (Stephens 1990b). Further, although cultural assumptions are largely inseparable not just from the discourse in which they are expressed but also from the language itself, dual language books, which can offer young readers an empowering kind of textual subjectivity, remain relatively rare. Because they are expensive to produce and the market is small, there is no likelihood that many will ever appear on a publisher's general list.

The principle aim in constructing a variety of subject positions for readers is to contribute towards a positive self-concept for children from minority groups, and to contribute to the social and personal development of *all* children by effacing notions of racial, class or gender superiority. There are two principal means for achieving this, and for both the concept of narrative focalization I discussed in Chapter 1 is of considerable significance, since both are concerned to depict social groups, values and customs without focalizing them through the perspective of a 'majority culture'. The first is to situate books entirely within the culture of a particular social group, representing its experience of the world and its own perception of that experience – in other words, its own subjectivity. Thus ordinary people can be represented in ordinary situations, not subjected to another culture's tendency to emphasize exceptional members or heroes of the group or to depict situations and life-styles as exotic, on the one hand, or stereotypical, on the other (see Banfield 1978 for an extended discussion of these principles). Reader subject positions will therefore be situated as if focalizing the text from within the group's assumptions.

A book which admirably achieves these objectives is *Mirandy and Brother Wind* (1988), by Patricia C. McKissack (text) and Jerry Pinkney (pictures). Set in the American South in about 1900, the book's account of Mirandy's attempts to capture the wind to partner her in a dancing competition (a cakewalk) is a strong recuperation of Black social history, particularly in its positive uses and depictions of Black English, cultural practices, and daily life (the latter especially in the pictures). The following extract clearly illustrates how some of these effects are achieved (for the purposes of subsequent discussion, I have coded sections according to whether they are narration [N], character focalization [F], or conversation [C]):

> [N] Following the creek downstream, Mirandy come to Mis Poinsettia's whitewashed cottage. [N/F?] Talk had it that Mis Poinsettia wasn't a for-real conjure woman like the ones in New Orleans. But didn't nobody mess with her, just in case talk was wrong.
>
> [N] Mis Poinsettia welcomed Mirandy inside. [C] 'Your people don't approve of conjure. Why come you here?' she say.
>
> [F] Mirandy figured if Mis Poinsettia was up on her conjure she ought to know why. But not wanting to 'pear sassy, she answered, [C] 'I need a potion to help me catch Brother Wind so he'll be my partner at the cakewalk.'
>
> (McKissack and Pinkney, *Mirandy and Brother Wind*, pp. 16–18)

The two main discoursal features which bear on subjectivity here are the shifts between forms characteristic of Black English and of Standard English, and the narrative shifts between narration, character focalization and conversational exchange as direct speech. Importantly, the narrative shifts do not coincide with code-switching between Black and Standard English; that is, Standard English is not restricted to narration any more than Black English is restricted to conversation. Thus a characteristic feature of Black English, that tense may be an optional category (Dillard 1972, pp. 49–52), will appear in the narration: the base form of the verb is used to describe a past action, as in 'Mirandy *come* to Mis Poinsettia's' (in place of Standard *came* or *comes*), and is also interspersed amongst the *inquit*-tags ('she *say*', but later 'she *answered*'). In fact, the structures of Black English are less prevalent within the conversations in this book than in the narration ('a for-real conjure woman', 'didn't no-body mess with her') or in character focalized stretches ('to 'pear sassy'). This is a key element in the dismantling of a traditional nar-rative strategy whereby narration is expressed in Standard English and only conversation includes the dialect or idiomatic register par-ticular to a social group; the effect of such a distribution is that idiomatic registers denote otherness as constructed from a majority-culture narrative perspective, and the stronger available subject position is thus that of the majority culture. In contrast, the subtle transitions between narration, focalization and conversation in *Mirandy and Brother Wind* enforce the dismantling of this strategy, because the strong subject position offered by the narration is cultu-rally identifiable with that of the focalizing character. This is particularly apparent in the second sentence, which cannot be clear-ly attributed to either narration or focalization, but represents a *communal* perception, both narratively and culturally.

The discoursal interpenetration of narration and conversation is not possible to the same extent in the second method used to con-struct alternative, now more multiple, subject positions, that is, through a portrayal of a society's multifariousness in its mixture of class and ethnic groups and its varied social practices. The principle here is rather to efface social differences in narration. The task can be carried out unobtrusively in picture books, because the dual mode can be exploited by simply representing cultural variety in the illustrations without addressing it in the text. This was a normal strategy in the Nippers series, which employed it in various ways. Geraldine Kaye's *Eight Days to Christmas* (1970), for example, which describes the production of a school Christmas pageant as related by one of the children, only points towards the classroom's multi-cultural mix through the children's names, and generally leaves it to the illustrations to encode multiculturalism covertly and to disclose that the story's first-person narrator is black. One might perhaps quibble that children such as 'Devi' and 'Depak' have possibly suf-fered some cultural subjection in taking part in this pageant, but be that as it may. A second way the Nippers books tried to minimize the dominance of a narrator's cultural perspective was to construct story mainly as conversation, as in Ronald Deadman's *The Preten-ders* (1972). Here a black child's reflection of his father's Jamaican origins is linguistically coded by two specific speech habits, the use of the vocative 'man' and of redundant final interrogatives ('see?', 'doesn't he?', 'isn't it?). More recently, non-explicit multiculturalism pervades such picture books as Janet and Allan Ahlberg's *The Clothes Horse* (1987) and *Starting School* (1988). In *Starting School*, for example, a group of children of varying ethnic and class backgrounds, and from various family situations, are represented in the normal processes involved with the very first term of school. There is now no linguistic representation of the group's considerable social mix and the unselfconscious multiculturalism of five-year-olds.

Fiction for older readers has also sought strategies to diminish the otherness of minority groups. Robert Leeson's *The Third Class Genie* (1975), for example, focalizes its comic fantasy narrative through Alec, a white child, but gives him experiences which almost imperceptibly shift his assumptions about the black children in his neighbourhood and school. Racism is represented as an adult ideological position which children learn. This is seen when, for instance, Alec denies a newspaper report of a 'Race riot' at his school: rather, 'It was just a punch-up, black against white' (Leeson, 1975, p. 60). The fine semantic distinction only foregrounds that the two perceptions have a common base. The book's thematic purpose is to dismantle hostilities grounded on the simple fact of otherness, as Alec and his black counterpart, 'Ginger', renegotiate their relationship from enmity to close friendship, and to show how such divisive prejudice is exploited by a society's self-interested power-seekers.

THE CONSTRUCTION OF THE 'SUBJECT' IN NARRATIVE FICTION

The negotiations between a reader and a text are analogous with the negotiations between a Self and an Other in actual world interpersonal discourse. The textual negotiations introduce an ideological dimension in the sphere of 'implied author' (the constructed writer-in-the-text, endowed with an orientation in time and space, an attitude, and even a personality) and 'implied reader' – a role implicit in the text which is equivalent to conventional social roles in the actual world. Benveniste (1971, pp. 225–6) argued that it is language itself which provides the possibility of subjectivity because it is language which enables a speaker to posit himself or herself as 'I': 'there is no other objective testimony to the identity of the subject except that which he himself thus gives about himself' (p. 226). It is in this sense that the 'meaning' of a text is situated not in the text itself, but in a reader's construction of it. But this is by no means as simple a situation as it appears, since if the subject is constituted within a structure of linguistic differentiations, it also follows that the subject is *inscribed* within language and can communicate only by conforming his or her speech to subject positions constituted within various discourse types. Fairclough points out that *subject* can signify not only the active role of 'the one causally implicated in action', but also one who is *subjected*, existing or being placed under the authority of another (Fairclough 1989, p. 39; see also Belsey 1980, Chapter 3). The implication for audiences of literary fictions is that they will, as part of the reading process, invoke an 'appropriate' subject position from past experience, which may correspond to a lesser or greater degree with experiences described in the text, or else they will either be inscribed as a subject position ready-made within the text or construct a subject position from materials to hand in the text. The sense in which the characteristically imprecise concept of the 'implied reader' is understood has an important bearing here. As Iser (1974) formulated it, the implied reader is what an interpretative act will pivot on, in that it mediates the meaning which is a potentiality inherent in a text's structures and the (real) reader's actualization of this potential. The 'implied' reader thus tends to blend into a notion of an 'ideal' reader, the reader who will best actualize a book's potential meanings. This latter sense is where Chambers, under the influence of Wayne Booth, took the concept in his 'The Reader in the Book' paper (1977), where he practically defines it as the totality of a particular text's linguistic choices, intertextual allusions, attitudes towards the social practices represented, and point of view. As I suggested in Chapter 1, the 'best' reading, as envisaged by this process, occurs when the real reader is most closely aligned with the ideological position of the implied reader. In practice this does not always happen, and neither is it always desirable. There are also special problems posed by texts which set out to deny any stable centre of potential meaning, and hence imply a reader capable of multiple perspectives.

Part of the socialization of the child is that she learns to operate as a subject within various discourse types, each of which establishes its particular set of subject positions, which in turn act as constraints upon those who occupy them (Belsey 1980, p. 61; Fairclough 1989, p. 102). These positions can be creative as well as created, in so far as an individual exists in a state of dialectic with social practice, and hence we can suppose a reading position which might be active or passive. Finally, and also crucial for any consideration of the relationship between reader roles and ideology, Fairclough (p. 103) observes that the process of socialization can be conceived of as the situating of people, over time, in a range of subject positions. The social subject is thus constituted as a particular configuration of positions, with the consequence that the subject is far less coherent and unitary than one might conclude by applying Benveniste's grammatical analogy in any straightforward way. An application to readers would then indicate various possibilities covering both the range of available subject positions and degrees of active or passive engagement.

Literary fictions reveal a curious doubleness about the subject position(s) of the implied reader. On the one hand, as Bakhtin argued, fiction is a dialogic mode without a specific centre of focus because it is, implicitly or explicitly, a mixture of discourse types (Jefferson 1980). This means that readers may select from a number of subject positions or occupy different subject positions in the course of the narrative. This is very apparent in, say, William Mayne's *Salt River Times* (1980), which constructs at least ten possible subject positions, and, it should be stressed, as many ideological positions (see Stephens 1992). Further, just as the subject within social practice is both agent of and object of discoursal processes, so discourse types within fiction are not just agents of representation but also objects of representation. The interaction of discourse types within narrative potentially, at least, allows them to be disclosed as self-regarding, narrow, fallible, and so on, hence permitting evaluation of the subject positions they imply. Viewed from this perspective, narrative becomes a polyphony of discourses, a self-reflexive and self-critical interplay of discourse types.

On the other hand, since these discourse types, as with social practices in the actual world, are concerned with positioning subjects they can also be ideologically powerful. The most important concept for children to grasp about literary fictions is always that of narrative point of view, since this has the function of constructing subject positions and inscribing ideological assumptions. No mode of narration can be devoid of ideology; ideology merely operates in different ways and is inscribed within texts slightly differently by each of the three principal narrating processes, as follows.

(1) *'Omniscient' narration*. A narrator either by direct address exerts

overt control over the reader (actually the implied reader or narratee), or by means of the apparent absence of a narrator implies that particular assumptions are a matter of common knowledge, shared between narrator and narratee. In particular, the way in which the existents of *story* (characters and setting) are presented may contribute towards the construction of an ethos (and hence ideology), and so may encode a societal ideology. This is particularly likely to be found in certain kinds of realism and in most historical fiction.

(2) *First-person narration.* This process inscribes ideology either (a) by strategically disclosing that the narrator is unreliable, whereby the text oppositionally constructs a world view, notions of what *is* right, or a right way of seeing and encoding; or, (b) by situating readers in a subject position effectively identical with that of the narrator, so that readers share the narrator's view of the world or are convicted of error when/if the narrator is proved to be in the wrong in any sense.

(3) *Focalization.* A subject position is frequently constituted as the same as that occupied by a main character from whose perspective events are presented, that is, readers identify with the character. The narrative strategy itself is now commonly referred to as *focalization.* I will discuss it in more detail below, in relation to the implied reader and to narrative structure more generally. For now, it is enough to say that in aligning themselves with a focalizing character, readers undergo textual subjection.

In both society and literature it appears that the individual strives for autonomous selfhood, and it is usual for narratives in children's literature to represent this striving as having a positive outcome. It is present in a heavily (and transparently) symbolic form in, say, the hope of attaining the state of 'self-winding' in Russell Hoban's *The Mouse and His Child* and in the comparable, though superficially more anarchic, *Wagstaffe the Wind-up Boy* (see Chapter 4, below), and it is acutely so in the vast number of children's books whose events take place in a world without adults, a narrative convention against which *Wagstaffe* is largely a satire. The message which the literature overwhelmingly communicates is that people ultimately wield their own subjectivity as the ground of their beliefs and actions. And this is the central tenet in the doctrine of the implied reader within reader response theories of reading.

THE IMPLIED READER IN CRITICAL PRACTICE

The implied reader became an important concept for discussion of children's literature for two main reasons. First, it was incorporated into some versions of so-called reader response criticism, which sought to break the power attributed to the text itself by the intrinsic criticism which dominated literary studies throughout the mid-twentieth century, and empower the reader instead. Implicit in this position is a rejection of the idea that successful reading is a specialized operation that demands specific knowledge of *how to read* a book. There is also sometimes a view expressed that children, especially young children, process texts differently from adults, though this view does not receive general assent (see Crago 1979, p. 145; Walsh 1983, p. 3). The second reason lies in a desire to find accessible entry-points into books and so to make them more palatable – to mediate them to their readers and help the readers to appreciate particular books and 'to become literary readers' (Chambers 1985, p. 37). Not all scholars interested in the area of reader response concern themselves with the theory of the implied reader, however, and the concept seems to be endemically absent from studies of reader response grounded in schema theory or cognitive development: see, for example, the special number of the *Journal of Research and Development in Education*, **16**, 3 (1983), where only one paper (Shavit) uses the concept, and then largely in a redirected historical sense. As a group, these studies seem to be essentially text-focused and committed to determinate meanings, perhaps as a consequence of their often prior interest in reading comprehension. The socialization aspect of text is also usually not taken up, despite the lead given by Applebee.

The investigation of reader responses is always a difficult area, and while an increasing number of studies is becoming available, they usually involve only a small number of participants and their findings must be regarded as conditional. Moreover, uncovering the actual impact of books on real readers is practically impossible, partly because there seems always to be a gap between having an experience and articulating it, a gap which may apply to adult readers as much as to children, and because the ideological component of response will frequently remain invisible. A glance through Kaye Webb's anthology *I Like This Poem*, for example, quickly reveals a range from intensely personal readings of poems ('Because it reminds me of . . .') to formulaic, classroom responses, indicators that in most cases the poems were met with, after all, in other anthologies and in mediated situations.

The incorporation of the implied reader into versions of reader-response criticism is not always useful. The varieties of critical practice bundled under the heading 'reader-response criticism' are so disparate as to render the term almost meaningless. It comprises at one extreme *text-focused* analyses which purport to explain how various literary strategies impact on 'the reader' (but which actually project the analyst's own responses onto a reified reader), and at the other extreme *reader-focused* ideas of processes by which readers transform elements of texts into figures for their own unconscious fantasies. I think the idea of the implied reader might be most useful if situated between these extremes, and if it is defined as an implied stance constructed out of a socially determined language in the context of some dominant social practices and inherent ideologies. If we accept Iser's argument that what brings a literary work into existence is the convergence of text and (real) reader (1974, p. 275), then the being or meaning of the text would be best characterized as a dialectic between textual discourse (including its construction of an implied reader and a range of potential subject positions) and a reader's disposition, familiarity with story conventions and experiential knowledge. This is the position I hold myself, and which I now want to examine through some analyses of the relation between reader and text: first, as it is witnessed in some children's ideological responses to two books obliquely about family breakup, and, second, in an investigation of some texts which complicate the dialectic between text and reader by insisting on their own indeterminacy.

IDEOLOGY AND THE IMPLIED READER IN TWO PICTURE BOOKS

In 1989 Susan Taylor and I analysed two recent picture-book versions of the Orcadian sealwife legend (Cooper and Hutton, *The Selkie Girl*, 1986; Gerstein, *The Seal Mother*, 1986) to determine the ideological positions which they implied or sought to inculcate and the crucial components of the narrative within which these positions became evident. The legend deals with initiative and power within marriage, though these reworkings of it focused more on the process of letting go of something which is an object of a strong desire. Each version preserves the ending in which the sealwife leaves husband and child(ren) to return to the sea. The books were read to 174 children at three Sydney schools to gauge their reactions to the values and attitudes expressed in the texts. The children were mainly from classes 6, 7 and 8 (that is, aged between ten and fourteen). The reading sessions were structured to promote comment about particular story events and components which we had previously identified as significant foci, but their procedure was also open enough to provide frequent opportunities for the children to express their spontaneous thoughts and reactions. The children were finally invited to offer some written responses and asked to 'rewrite the story' they had heard from the point at which the hiding - place of the sealskin was discovered by one of the sealwife's children. We investigated five main loci for the ideology surrounding marriage, but I will restrict my remarks here to a summary of our findings concerning only one of these, the departure of the mother, basing my comments on the protocols rewriting the endings.

Both picture books offer ameliorated endings, compared with more traditional versions. Cooper/Hutton allow the whole family an annual meeting with the selkie in her human form, and Gerstein allows Andrew unlimited access to his mother during his childhood and then an ongoing tradition of a Midsummer's Eve family gathering. It is no longer a strange notion that a family's happiness might exist more fully outside traditional marriage, in some arrangement which allows women more personal freedom, but it remains less ideologically acceptable within society, which still looks askance at the suggestion that the individual's rights to selfhood and happiness might transcend duty to family within a conventional organization. This is particularly evident in the Cooper/Hutton book, in which the selkie is rendered abject by an act committed against her which deprives her of her identity and of her place in society, and substitutes another identity and place for them; the book goes on to suggest that if marriage is like that, then in turn its organizations and systems will have to be overturned.

In each book the ideal implied reader is a child aware of the possibility of parental separation who will accede to the child characters' acceptance of their changed situation after some process of adjustment. There are more possible subject positions, however, and they are more complex, since the obvious ones – association with the child characters – do not emerge until the narratives are well under way. Before this, readers have the very complicated situation of the subject positions within the rather abrupt courtship, in which male desire overrides female autonomy. To this extent, then, the books may be understood to deal with a struggle for autonomy. The situation is particularly complex in the Cooper/Hutton version, since the early point of view represented is largely that of the subjugating male, not the female. Gerstein's one child has to work through the process of letting go for himself, while Cooper/Hutton explore the situation through two possible subject positions, represented by an older, female child willing to let go and an unwilling younger, male child whose final acceptance is only expressed implicitly.

We expected that the changes, additions and emphases made by the children in the rewritings would indicate their degree of engagement with the text, the aspects of the narrative that aroused their interest or concern, their values and attitudes relevant to those textual components, and whether differences (if any) in the responses were associated with the gender of the respondents. Significantly, a common change was to transform the mode of narration from third person to first person, and this often seemed to reflect a very strong personal involvement with the story, to the point at times where Gerstein's male child has clearly become a female character.

(a) Rewriting *The Seal Mother*

Where substantive changes were made to the ending, they converged in a number of shared plots which revealed a striking divergence between male and female participants. Thus an outcome constructed by many female participants involved a reconstruction of the story which strengthened the motif of mother–child bonding, so that they live together permanently in the underwater world (with varying degrees of rejection, and sometimes punishment, of the man). Such re-workings seem to indicate that some female readers functioned not in alignment with the text's implied reader but from their own subjectivity and desire for self-determination.

Male participants tended to favour one of four different outcomes.

(1) The child returns the skin, but the mother does not leave. Either

the skin had lost its power, or the mother decides to opt for land and family life.

(2) The man is confronted with a mother–son bond and reacts violently against it; this may result in the death of the mother, or of both mother and child.

(3) The child finds the skin, but either delays returning it until he has reached adulthood (and no longer needs a mother!) or uses his possession of the skin to bargain with his mother and impose conditions on his returning it: she must visit frequently; she must take him with her. Only one writer recognized that he was replicating the father's original appropriation of the woman.

(4) A frequently selected conclusion (but selected *only* by males) is the destruction of the skin, either accidentally or deliberately. Some of these responses were startlingly violent, and even envisaged the death of the mother with the destruction of the skin. The inherent irony in this latter response, of course, is that rather than allow the mother freedom and self-determination at the expense of her bond to the child, the writer is prepared to kill the mother and lose her anyway. There is, however, perhaps a sense here that the pain of the mother's death is commensurate with, if not preferable to, the pain of losing her.

(b) Rewriting *The Selkie Girl*

While there were some parallels between the rewritings of each text, there were also some significant differences which foregrounded or reflected variations in ideological formation between the two. *The Selkie Girl* has the less obviously recuperative ending, and this was subjected to differences of emphasis: in some reworkings it was played down, so that more emphasis fell on the sorrow and resignation of husband and children; in others, however, it was emphasized more strongly, focusing on the contact between the family members, the continuation of a maternal protective role, or the strength and perceptiveness of the daughter. These responses obviously reflect the desire of their authors for positive outcomes and relationships, and in some cases suggest an understanding, at least intuitive, that daughter and mother share in a growth in selfhood and exhibit an empowering female bonding.

A major difference between the rewritings of the two versions was an almost complete absence of a retributive element in the re-versions of *The Selkie Girl* (only one example). We surmised that this difference derives from an absence of antagonism and overt conflict earlier in the Cooper/Hutton text, and the depiction of the man as gentler than Gerstein's man. Once again a significant proportion of male children produced an outcome whereby the sealskin, and hence the selkie's chance of freedom, was destroyed. We read the Cooper/Hutton ending as achieving a socially positive balance, and this reading is perhaps confirmed in so far as this group was in-clined to construct the story so that the skin is destroyed by accident or even by newly introduced characters, thus preventing the selkie's children from being implicated in its (or in one example, her) des-truction. So while some male participants still construct outcomes which contain the mother, they seem to do so under the influence of the more general sense of satisfaction with the book's original ending, which was recognized as balanced, if not entirely happy.

An essential difference between the two books, in our reading, is that the Cooper/Hutton reworks the old legend in the context of an awareness that the tradition of children's literature has been tied to particular forms of dominance and of family organization, and since those forms no longer successfully structure late twentieth-century society they can no longer be honestly used to structure its lit-erature. Gerstein, though, uses a traditional idea of mother–son bonding to remove the element of crisis from his story. This to us is a pity, since the book seems to share with Cooper/Hutton an inten-tion to use the legend, and hence marriage, to represent **all** Self/Other relationships in family and society – hence the important changes in the roles given to the children in these versions: to per-ceive that the mother has an independent being and to let her go is to achieve a sense of object/person permanence which marks the child's maturation beyond an egocentric relationship with the world. As is to be expected, many of the students who participated in our study showed themselves to be entering such a stage. But these are not always comfortable processes, as many participants recognized through *The Selkie Girl*'s acknowledgment of the pain in-volved in realizing the potential. Many other participants, especially males, recoiled in something akin to horror at the spectre of loss and its effect on them. The responses clearly offer plenty of scope for speculation about different patterns of socialization in Australian society, and well illustrate how a reader's situation within an ideological practice can prompt resistance to alignment with a subject position constructed for an implied reader.

IMPLICATION AND INFERENCE – READER AND TEXT

The data collected from readers reading the sealwife stories suggested some interesting conclusions about the relationship between ideology, subject position and implied reader. Readers not only arrived at the same 'story' from each book but also inferred a common 'significance', that is, that the narrative was not just a sad story about a man and a sealwife (the conclusion of readers who do not move on to significance) but about marital separation and power relationships. Eleven-year-olds were as capable of inferring this as were thirteen-year-olds. The books' socializing objectives, however, were met with both full complicity and quite violent rejection, so even if (real) audiences were prepared to adopt the subject position of the implied reader it was not the inevitable outcome that they also adopted the ideological frame implicit in that position. It also seemed to be the case that readers could refuse that subject position and still actively engage with the texts, apparently constructing a subject position from within their everyday social practice in order to oppose the position implied by the text. This option has clear ideological implications, in that it indicates the selection of a more socially conservative position, and might be taken as a reflection of the differing socializing practices applied to boys and girls in Australian society (though there are also many other differences at this age level). The Cooper/Hutton version, in particular, constructed the narrative around an acute moral dilemma – should the woman take back the freedom and happiness she had lost when this might impact adversely on her children? – and implicitly required readers to make a considerable altruistic gesture in allowing her that freedom. Many, as might be expected, were not willing to do this, but presumably the authors would find some satisfaction in having induced readers to contemplate the possibility at all.

Readers are implicated in narrative by inferring significance from discourse and by evaluating the choices characters must make between different courses of action. Theories of the implied reader also argue that the reader is 'drawn into' or implicated in the text by the need to fill many small-scale information 'gaps' as well: to make inferences, to decode figurative utterances and to construct characters on the basis of the information given in the text. Such gaps are exemplified in the passage below, which occurs in *The Selkie Girl* at the point just after the man had stolen the sealwife's skin and hence captured her. I have identified seven inferences which readers must draw, and have numbered the sequences accordingly:

[1] So Donallan married the selkie girl, and they lived together in the croft with the dog and the cat, and the sheep outside grazing the hills. [2] She would not tell him her true name, so he called her Mairi. [3] He kept her sealskin hidden, [4] checking it often to make sure it never cracked or dried out. [5] After the first day, she never asked for it again.

[6] Mairi worked as hard as Donallan on the croft, and because he was gentle and loving, she no longer wept. When their first child was born, he saw her smile. But he never heard her sing again, [7] and each year when the seventh day of the flood tides came round, he would find her looking sadly out at the sea, with her head tilted as if she were listening.

(Cooper and Hutton, *The Selkie Girl*, pp. 20–1)

Likely inferences to be drawn are something like this:

(1) The sealwife accommodates herself to a human (and therefore alien) lifestyle.
(2) She does not really accept this situation, but it is imposed upon her, like the name.
(3) She would leave if she could.
(4) Her well-being depends on the condition of the skin. Readers can infer that this implies (a) her physical well-being, or continued survival; and/or (b) her mental and emotional well-being. Further, (c) the skin symbolizes whatever keeps a person in an undesirable situation – this last being an inference implicating the larger significance of the narrative.
(5) There is a complex gap here. Readers may infer that (a) she has accepted her lot or (b) she is biding her time. To infer simply the former would probably be a contextual misreading, since an awareness of textual coherence would recognize that the inference drawn at 5 is apt to be conditioned by the inferences drawn at 2, 3 and 4. An appropriate inference would incorporate both (a) and (b).
(6) Again a complex process of inferencing. Inferences 6 and 7

together repeat inferences 1–3. Inference 6 is initially complicated by the explicit cause-effect stretch in 'because he . . . she no longer', but the ameliorative element is offset by the implications of the series: '-wept | +smile | -sing' (compare inference 2).

(7) The end of the sequence may function inferentially as a summation of all the preceding inferences.

The process of inference-making is an aspect of how a reader moves around amongst discourse, story and significance, and inferences themselves are thus broadly of two kinds, those that bear on story and those that bear on significance. But the two are not always separable, and theorists suggest that in making the former, readers are implicitly led to make the latter: by becoming implicated in story, they become implicated in significance. If, by making inferences, readers bring assumptions into the process of interpretation, the text exerts power over them by making them entertain such assumptions in order to make sense of the text (Fairclough 1989, p. 83). Aidan Chambers envisaged the function of gaps in narrative as part of the way an author 'leads the reader towards possible meaning(s); and he stage-manages the reader's involvement by bringing into play various techniques which he knows influence the reader's responses and expectations' (Chambers 1985, p. 46). I have already remarked earlier that an implication of this position is that such inferencing entails the reader's internalization of the text's implicit ideologies. Chambers argues from an assumption of determinate meanings and uses such formulations as 'the book's true meaning' (p. 56). Wolfgang Iser, who was Chambers' primary inspiration, did not. Iser (1974) argued that inferences were a matter of choices, and in excluding some possibilities a reader constructs a meaning which includes only parts of the text's potential, and so there can be no determinate readings. Chambers' model is much more text-focused, and really only empowers the reader to find what the writer wants found. Writing of the major gap in Sendak's *Where the Wild Things Are* (that is, that Max's experience is a dream) he suggests it is 'so vital that, unless the reader fills it, the profound meaning of the book cannot be discovered' (1985, p. 48). From one perspective, the attitude is praiseworthy in that it envisages children producing 'better' readings and developing their interest in books. But this should not be argued so as to exclude the other perspective, that the process involves social values as well as reading strategies. The responses to the sealwife stories indicate the important role played by ideology in reading, and those responses coming from ideological positions hostile to those of the texts, rejecting the role of the implied reader, cannot be dismissed as invalid, whether or not we choose to regard them as more or less deplorable misreadings, or as reflections of deplorable social practices.

The effacing of the ideological implication is a blind spot in Chambers' account of the implied reader. There are also two other turns in the argument which I would consider to be wrong moves with respect to the relation between the implied reader and the ideology of text. First, apparently because the overall theory of narrative is not delicate enough, he conflates implied author and focalizer. The section on 'point of view' equates 'putting at the centre of the story a child through whose being everything is seen and felt' and the reader finding 'an implied author whom he can befriend because he is of the tribe of childhood as well' (p. 42). When, in his later discussion of *The Children at Green Knowe*, he suggests that the story is effectively told by Mrs Oldknow, he builds the distinction back into his theory. Second, while he recognizes that some authors employ strategies 'deliberately designed to alienate the reader from the events and from the people described' (p. 44), his inclination is to reject such strategies unless they also enable the reader to find a subject position in alignment with story existents. This is because his own ideology of reading demands a reified 'implicated' reader, led by textual strategies to discover a determinate meaning. The two arguments are interrelated. I wish to argue that the kind of subject position described here as alienated can be an empowered position. I shall begin, though, with the question of focalizers and subject positions.

FOCALIZERS AND SUBJECT POSITIONS

Since in presenting their imaginary versions of social relationships in the actual world, fictional narratives are imbued with ideology, a key part of the outworking of ideology is then the situating of readers, who, in taking up a position from which the text is most readily intelligible, are apt to be situated within the frame of the text's ideology; that is, they are subjected to and by that ideology (see Belsey 1980, pp. 56–7). The position the reader occupies is sometimes that of the narrator, but it is also frequently defined by that of a main character from whose perspective events are presented. This character perspective, or focalization, has some implications crucial for reader response, the implied reader and ideological practices.

In aligning themselves with a focalizing character, readers match their own sense of selfhood with ideas of self constructed in and by the text, not principally because of the inherent nature of events and characters described, but through the mode through which these are perceived. Thus a crucial textual distinction, broadly put, is between narratives which encourage readers to adopt a stance which is identical with that of either the narrator or the principal focalizer, and narratives which incorporate strategies which distance the reader (by showing, for example, a separation between narrator-perception and focalizer-perception, as when it is obvious to readers that a focalizing character is misinterpreting an event or situation). This is not an either/or distinction, but a matter of degree across a spectrum. The difference is important for the kind of reading self a reader will construct for the purposes of a particular text. Total identification with the focalizer is a strategy for reading which is widely encouraged in schools, and few people have questioned its appropriateness as a strategy (but see Nodelman 1981, pp. 180–1; Zipes 1983, p. 52). If a function of children's literature is to socialize its readers, identification with focalizers is one of its chief methods, since by this means, at least for the duration of the reading time, the reader's own selfhood is effaced and the reader internalizes the perceptions and attitudes of the focalizer and is thus reconstituted as a subject within the text. Further, as discourse analysts have pointed out with relation to schema theory, any attempt to alter the mental state of another human being is most successful where there is already a coincidence between mental states, and the alteration achieved is only minimal (Cook 1989, p. 74). This perhaps also partly explains why the sealwife books evoked such hostile reactions from some readers. In my view, the present habit of stressing reader-focused approaches to text in combination with advocacy of identification with focalizers, inconsistent as this combination may be, is a dangerous ideological tool and pedagogically irresponsible. It fosters an illusion that readers are in control of the text whereas they are highly susceptible to the ideologies of the text, especially the unarticulated or implicit ideologies.

Reading establishes a relationship between the reader and a

potential alter ego, the focalizer(s), but also a relationship between the reader and the reader's own selfhood, prompted by such responses to the text as: do I feel that way? Is this like my school (or family, or friends etc.)? What would I do in this situation? It is crucial at this point of the argument to insist once more that texts do not exist in a vacuum, but are context-dependent. They are produced within, and to an extent by, particular social formations, and they seek, explicitly or implicitly, to inculcate particular social values and attitudes available at the time of production. If readers can maintain a dual orientation (that is, towards self and towards focalizer), then, it seems reasonable to suggest, they will be engaging with a structured form of the larger process whereby the self negotiates its own coming into being in relation to society. That is, reading re-enacts the process through which an individual constructs a social self through the interaction of the ego and the social formation.

Unqualified identification with focalizers attributes a coherent reality and objectivity to the world constructed by the text. Berger and Luckmann (1966, p. 38) argued that the act of speaking 'crystallizes the speaker's own subjectivity' and reconfirms selfhood. I would suggest that the process I am describing purports to do just that through the reader's acts of perception, but instead constructs a false subjectivity and a selfhood which is actually mimetic of the focalizing selfhood in the text. Readers remain unaware that their perceptions and attitudes are being conditioned by this process. Distancing strategies, on the other hand, encourage the constitution of a reading self in relation to the other constituted in and by the text. This alternative process does not guarantee freedom from conditioning, since a position separate from the focalizer may well merely represent the ideological position of narrator (and then perhaps author). To respond to a main character's actions with, say, 'But that's not right at all! What's really happening is that . . .', may only be to infer a position obliquely inherent in the text and which communicates a message all the more powerful just because the reader has discovered it. As Fairclough points out (1989, p. 85), ideology is most effective when its workings are least visible. A reader's self may be subjected by a text both through identification with a focalizer, whose attitudes will seem unexceptionable, and through a disclosed, common-sense 'discovery', which flatters the reader's own perceptiveness. Both processes may therefore function ideologically. The optimum enabling state for the reader is to have a number of available reading strategies, including an interrogative engagement with the implied reader.

ESTRANGED SUBJECT POSITIONS

There are many strategies by which readers may be 'estranged' from the possibility of simple identification, and so prevented from adopting a single subject position, and these function with different degrees of severity. They include: shifts in focalizer; focalizers who are not 'nice people', and hence do not invite reader identification; multi-stranded narration, which may play one significance against another; intertextual allusiveness, which may indicate the presence of more than one interpretative frame and require top-down reading; metafictional playfulness, whereby a text draws attention to its own status and processes as a fiction; and overtly inscribed indeterminacies. I will deal with most of these in the course of this book, so will consider here only a couple of examples which can be discussed within the context of the narratological frame outlined above in Chapter 1.

A primary supposition about story is that its narrator does not have to tell the truth. As a remark about a literary work this is almost too obvious to bother with, though a narrator who flaunts mendacity will deny readers a comfortable subject position. The potential difference between truth claims and truth value in a text does serve as a reminder that the text mediates a contract between author and reader which can take a great number of forms, and a reader's orientation towards the text will be affected, and even directed, by the terms of the contract. In children's literature the possible contractual parameters are slightly more restricted than in fiction writing in general, in that extreme types of metafictional strategies are virtually absent. The parameters are, I think, these: at one end, the author may construct narrative which invites reading 'as if' it were a documentary transcription of events in the actual world, whereby the implied reader reconstructs an experience which corresponds with the experience of the characters within it; at the other end, the author may insist on the textuality of the text, drawing attention both to authorial manipulation and the processes by which readers interpret the fictive world in terms of the actual world. The former type – text 'as if it were the actual world' – is characteristic of contemporary realism and most historical fiction, and it is quite common for publishers of such books to pre-empt the reader's subject position by asserting or implying an actual world status for the narrative: 'based on a true story', 'real life drama', and so on. Such narratives virtually efface any consciousness that stories and their significance are reassembled by readers on the basis of the discourses available to them. The latter type – self-conscious textuality – implies a reader whose role is that of author's playmate, sharing a game with deducible rules, and being a little more conscious of the way meanings are both linguistically and socially constructed.

THE DIALECTIC OF READING AS PLAY

The contract which is grounded on a playful relationship between implied author and implied reader, and permits actual readers to read playfully, more generally illustrates the nature of literary textuality. A pertinent example here is to be found in the title of and story onsets in Susan Price's collection of stories *Here Lies Price* (1987). The very title of the book is an important part of the author/reader game because play has started before the book is even opened. In its three words the title incorporates an almost dazzling array of multiple, contradictory meanings, not all of which, it should be noted, will be available to all readers – the title is radically indeterminate. Even the locative adverb 'here' functions as both a close proximal deictic and an unspecifying proximal deictic. Possibilities are:

(1) It is a traditional tombstone inscription (the dust-jacket of the first edition depicts a ghoulish figure in a graveyard). Thus

Here	*Lies*	*Price*
locative adverb	physical	person
(unspecifying deictic)	passive	
actual world reference		

(2) It announces the author's act of fabulation: story-telling as untruth. Thus

Here	*Lies*	*Price*
locative adverb	verbal	person
(close proximal deictic)	active	
textual reference		
'this book'		

(3) It parodies a publisher's blurb, proclaiming the worth of the text, by having recourse to an archaic signification of *price* 'value, worth'. The reader is left to infer, however, whether the basis of worth is because the stories are traditional or 'found' stories, or because of the literary merit of these particular versions. Thus

Here	*Lies*	*Price*
locative adverb	physical	value marker
(close proximal deictic)	passive	'of cultural worth'
textual reference		'of literary merit'
'this book'		

(4) Consistent with (1) and (3), but contradictory to (2), the title announces the post-structuralist 'death' of the author, or, in a more accessible context, it mockingly declares the effacement of the author when the text 'merely' reinscribes the actual world. This is a joke, since while the stories claim to do this, none does (nor does any story, of course), and therefore (2) applies here after all. Thus

Here	*Lies*	*Price*
locative adverb	[verbal	person
(unspecifying deictic)	active	
close proximal	[physical	
textual reference	passive	
'this book'		

As a discrete utterance, 'Here Lies Price' thus has many meanings but no singular determinate meaning. Meaning has to be determined by context but, as the above analysis indicates, more than one context, and more than one kind of context, is involved. As the title of a published artefact it is given one kind of material context, but readers bring to it various kinds of actual world knowledge, presuppositions about the nature of texts, and, in some cases, specialized knowledge of diachronic semantics and of the more arcane discourses of literary and narrative theory. Therefore there can be for this text neither a single implied reader nor a simple identifiable subject position from which a real reader might engage with the text. Singularity is dissolved in multi-faceted play.

Price teases out such implications and sustains the multiple perspective by beginning each story with some statement dealing with the truth value of the story in relation to the actual world and its conventions for assuming truthfulness. Here are some of the openings:

[1] Here's a true story about liars.

[2] This is a true story because it happened to my great-grandfather

[3] I know that this must be a true story, because I read it in a book.

[4] This story is so true, you'll be told it in a dozen pubs.

[5] This is a story about Jesus, so it must be true.

[6] This is a true story because I say so.

[7] I visited a school and met a boy named Jason, who told me this story.

   [Here the truth claim is foregrounded by being left implicit, authenticated by story existents as in realist fiction. This is the only story onset in which this happens.]

(Price, *Here Lies Price*, Story onsets)

The truth value of a narrative, it is thus asserted, lies in various kinds of authority: actual world (2, 6), textual (3), supernatural (5), intersubjectivity (7), and common knowledge (4). The first example, however, does not attempt to authenticate its truth value, offering instead a paradox about truth and untruth as an introduction to a traditional story which embeds another traditional story within it. Readers are thus prepared to be sceptical about subsequent assertions of truthfulness and to enter into the game of constructing fictions and exploring the discoursal implications of narrative fiction. The story onsets as a group constitute an engaging (and instructive) conversation with readers about epistemology and the grounding of authority, about literary types, and about the relationships between art and reality and between readers and texts.

INSCRIBED INDETERMINACY

Children's literature, it will come as no surprise, orientates itself towards a commonplace neatly formulated by Berger and Luckmann

(1966, p. 33): 'Everyday life presents itself as a reality interpreted by men [sic] and subjectively meaningful to them as a coherent world.' Much, perhaps most, early writing for children sought to assert meaning within a very particular interpretation of reality, situating its texts within a dominant religious, moral, social and economic world-view. The impulse to do this still exists, though theories of reality and world-views are now generally more pluralistic, and it is even permissible to explore the very basis of thinking about reality. It can now be said that a theory of reality is a way of ordering the world so as to render it intelligible, and it is possible to explore, in this context, the ambiguities of Berger and Luckmann's 'subjective-ly' – constructing a subject through interaction with the 'world', interpreting the world solipsistically as an extension of the self.

Some particularly interesting forays into questions of the subject and of constructed intelligibility have been made by the Australian writer Jenny Wagner in picture books accessible to a pre-school audience. In *The Bunyip of Berkeley's Creek* (illustrated by Ron Brooks), she explores George Berkeley's Subjective Idealist theory of reality (that is, reality inheres in ideas, and belongs to the subject who has those ideas). The bunyip, a creature from Australian Aboriginal legend, in a quest for its own subjectivity suffers through Berkeley's precept that to exist is to be perceived. Since everybody he questions classifies *bunyip* in terms of their own ordering of reality, including 'Bunyips don't exist', the bunyip is unable to enter into intersubjectivity and his own 'bunyip-ness' is never perceived until he meets another bunyip. Again, in *John Brown, Rose and the Midnight Cat* (also with Brooks as collaborator), the two characters inside the house, Rose and her dog, John Brown, differ initially as to whether the cat outside exists or not, and then as to what it sig-nifies. This difference extends to the book's larger significance as well, resulting in an indefinite deferral of 'meaning' which has made this one of the most argued-about picture books produced in Australia. The effect of indeterminacy is further intensified by the implied audience position, in that both verbal and visual strategies preclude more than a momentary audience alignment with any of the book's three characters.

The book I am going to discuss in some detail is *The Machine at the Heart of the World* (1983), illustrated by Jeff Fisher. For this book Wagner has turned to the philosophy of Thomas Hobbes, which, in its assertions that all actions are determined by a desire for power, and its argument that the world can only be ordered by a social contract based on self-interest and authoritarianism, seems very pertinent both to social practice in late-twentieth-century societies and to my particular concern with subjectivity. Perhaps more than in the other two books, meaning (or its deferral) is here a product of interaction between verbal text and illustration. The book's 'story' is as follows: the world is run by a machine operated at its centre; entropy sets in, and a result is that the machine's existence is discovered, and it is taken over and operated in order to advance sectional economic and political interests; the result is chaos, until Theobald, the machine's proper operator, resumes control and restores order. The significance of the book is rather elusive, in that it seems both to offer a plenitude of meaning and to be devoid of meaning at its own centre. That is, the machine at the heart of the world is an unsignifying sign: a Christian might assert that Theobald is a figure for God, so that when human beings displace God from his role the world collapses into chaos (though this reading sits uncomfortably with the order of events, since the process originates with entropy: 'But one day he began to grow tired, and the machine began to run down. No one in the world noticed it, only Theobald'); a materialist could assert that the world operates mechanistically, and its problems are caused by economic greed and the desire by those in power to aggrandize themselves. The 'world' which 'Theobald ran' with his machine is patently a symbol. It is like the world readers are familiar with, in that it has some social and economic structures reminiscent of parts of Earth; but the machine itself is a replica of the 'world' of which it sits at the centre, and there is a cause–effect, microcosm–macrocosm relationship between the two worlds.

The inscribing of indeterminacy begins with the opening double-page spread (see Plate 3): the reader as viewer is situated above Theobald's domain, looking straight down but well off-centre. The effect is that of looking at a model on a sphere, so that there are neither vertical planes nor a 'right' side up: moreover, because no plane lies at right angles to the bottom edge of the book, the reader feels compelled to turn the book through 360 degrees in order to construct a point of view, but can never see the picture as a whole, only ever managing to focus on whatever segment happens to be approximately vertical at any time – a reminder that reality is perceived as fragments and has no inherent essential order. Finally, from every viewing position the point of convergence remains as a representation of infinity, the dark patch into which all pillars de-

Plate 3 *The Machine at the Heart of the World*

scend and disappear. What this picture displays is a collage world assembled from *bricolage*, from found objects, and the machine itself is also a collage (as it must be, if it is to be a microcosm of a constructed reality). Australian adults might recognize in the machine an allusion to the 1970s cartoons of Bruce Petty commenting on Australian socio-political life. But children will see in it all the fantasy machines of their own devising. All of these elements decentre meaning at the outset of the book, so by the time the machine is seen in close-up and in operation (pp. 8–9), and Theobald is shown as an aging man wearing a shabby suit, a striped apron, a nightcap and pink sneakers, comic fantasy in the illustrations operates in conflict with the flat certitudes of the text:

> From his machine he made the weather, helped the plants grow, controlled the tides and kept the stars in their places.
>   Theobald ran the world.
>   (Wagner and Fisher, *The Machine at the Heart of the World*, pp. 8–9)

It seems to me that such a narrative situation simultaneously throws the audience back on whatever notions of reality they use to make sense of the world and denies any absolute validity to that reality.

At first glance the book's ending appears facile: Theobald takes over the machine again, and the world is put to rights, though the leaky roof that started the trouble is not mended. Theobald has apparently taken on an apprentice, the boy who first discovered and revealed Theobald's existence and his machine to the world, and thereby caused the trouble – but then did he? The final cause is another indeterminacy, and the book offers many possibilities: the entropic process itself; Theobald's tiredness; the unmended leak; the boy's disclosure of how the world worked; the greed of people wanting to work the world for their own benefit. Even the turning-point is indefinite: it may be the boy's economic need (he needs the grass to grow so he can mow the lawn and earn his pocket money), or it may be his offer to help Theobald in return for having the machine started again.

Further, the failure of closure in meaning is reflected structurally in the book's allusion to cyclical form without strictly rendering it. That is, while entropy has been arrested, in that Theobald has returned to work, has help, and is dressed more colourfully (including a beanie instead of a nightcap), this is only temporary, since the world is only returned to the point at which it had begun to run down, as is suggested by the reminiscence of page 10 in the narrative's closing words:

> He noticed that the roof was leaking.
> I'll fix that one day,' he said.
> He put buckets under the drips and went on pedalling.
>
> (p. 10)

> The boy helped to empty the buckets,
> but Theobald's roof was still leaking.
> 'I'll fix it some day,' he said.
>
> (Wagner and Fisher, *The Machine at the Heart of the World*, p. 28)

The Machine at the Heart of the World can bear a still more elaborated, more intertextual, reading, however. In Chapter 6 I will consider some examples of historical fiction which argue that causality is not inherent in time and events but represents an ordering imposed retrospectively. This book is similar in its relationship with Hobbesian empiricism: that is, the view that human life is driven by matter and motion, and human actions by immediate self-interest. Thus at the centre of the book is the world's response to the boy's information:

> 'There's a machine at the heart of the world,' he [the Mayor] said.
> 'We can have everything we want.'
>
> The farmers wanted more wheat, the builders wanted more timber,
> the fishermen wanted more fish, and the Mayor wanted fine weather
> for The Parade.
>
> (Wagner and Fisher, *The Machine at the Heart of the World*, pp. 12, 14)

The crucial gap here is in the false causal relationship between the two parts of the Mayor's utterance, since, obviously enough, a mechanistic universe is not a guarantee of an infinite fulfilment of desire. Here is the limit to the subject's self-construction as an ego-driven exercise of power. That the illustrations depict the Mayor as a ridiculous, parodic isomorph of Napoleon Bonaparte reinforces the point. The view that all actions are determined by the desire for power is also called into question, first by the role of Theobald, who relinquishes control of the machine without resistance and only re-assumes it reluctantly, and then by the consequences of the egoistic exercise of power – social and economic chaos in a boom-and-bust cycle. In this way, the book becomes a fairly transparent allegory about capitalist economic systems crudely based on private sector growth and the claim that what is good for business (and can be conspicuously exploited by government) is good for the people as a whole.

I suggested above that there is no altruism at work in the boy's actions, and want now to look at the scene in which he proposes what is in effect a social contract to Theobald, a proposal quite reminiscent of Hobbes' social contract based on self-interest. Here is the scene:

> 'You can go away, too,' said Theobald.
> 'You're the one who started all this.'
> 'I just wanted to tell you,' said the boy, 'that your drip buckets need
> emptying. I'll empty them for you if you like – if you start your machine
> again.'
>
> (Wagner and Fisher, *The Machine at the Heart of the World*, p. 24)

The two speakers use quite different linguistic structures. Theobald's utterance depends on implicit cause-and-effect linking, but the demand on the audience to make the desired inference may also prompt a moment of hesitation in which to recollect that the final cause is not so easily determined. It is, furthermore, a statement which seeks to preclude an answer. The boy's response is to break the implicit injunction to silence and with it the conversational principle of relation, and to make a tightly cohesive utterance which develops from a position of near abasement to one of power. The first head clause, with its effacing qualifier 'just', is little more than phatic, as the force of the utterance resides rather in the repetitions of 'empty(-)' and the climactic and contrastive doubling of conditional clauses:

the polite 'if you like'

the negotiative demand 'if you start your machine again'.

The pragmatic consequence of this negotiation is a form of utilitarianism whereby co-operation produces a good for the greater number of people. In this reading, the unpatched hole in the ceiling becomes an ambiguous sign: it is a reminder that the cycle can be repeated; it enables a repetition of the cycle.

To pursue a reading of *The Machine at the Heart of the World* this far raises some particular problems. An audience must read the illustrations at least as vigorously as the verbal text because the latter cannot in itself disclose the book's full potential as a signifying discourse. It is possible to construct a reading of the book as a socio-economic allegory without any intertextual reference to Thomas Hobbes (which children obviously do not have available) or to Napoleon, but this still means that the book signifies in a number of different ways according to the kinds of readers it has and the kinds of construction of significance those readers will make. Even within the more elaborate frame, a Christian and a materialist will construct different interpretations of the central function of Theobald, and are certain to make different constructions of the social contract between Theobald and the boy which gets the machine working again. So while the book seems to suggest that there is a natural and inherent order in the world, represented by the proper functioning of the machine, the meaning of the machine will remain indeterminate and variously interpreted in a way appropriate to the ideological presuppositions of the audience.

CONCLUSION

Chapter 2 may be summed up in a recapitulation of the following premises and conclusions.

The subject/individual exists within a dialectical relationship with sociality as configured *moments* of interpretation within the social relations which produce the subject and which the subject helps to produce. The relationship between a subject's activities as a reader and a work of fiction which is the object of the reading both replicates other forms of subject–sociality interactions, in so far as the relationship between a reader and a text is dialectical, and constructs a specular form of those interactions, since a work of fiction mirrors the picturations and narratives which the subject draws upon for its own sense of selfhood. The subject as reader is thus confronted with numerous textual examples in which a fictive character is constructed intersubjectively, and hence with models for variously constructing a subject through interaction with the 'world', interpreting the world solipsistically as an extension of the self, or interpreting the self as a mere product of sociality.

Narrative fictions have referential meaning and are constructed with the intent of shaping reader responses, and hence reader attitudes. A fictive text might offer its readers a variety of possible interpretative subject positions, ranging from the passive to the interrogative. These differences are of crucial importance for reading fiction, and especially for examining the possibility of ideological impact on readers. An ideological dimension enters the negotiations between a reader and a text especially through the constructed sphere of the 'implied reader' – a role implicit in the text which is equivalent to conventional social roles in the actual world. The concept of the implied reader is most useful if it is situated between the extremes of text-focused and reader-focused approaches, and if it is defined as an implied stance constructed out of a socially determined language in the context of some dominant social practices and inherent ideologies.

The *subject* can signify not only the role of one who acts, but also one who is *subjected* to the authority of the text. Readers may thus invoke a personal subject position separate from the text, or be inscribed as a subject position ready-made within the text, or construct a more interrogative subject position on the basis of the text. Just as the subject is constituted in sociality as a particular configuration of positions, so readers may be constituted by a range of available positions, and may select from a number of subject positions or occupy different subject positions in the course of the narrative.

The meaning of a text is constituted as a dialectic between textual discourse and a reader's pre-existing subjectivity. For the purposes of this dialectic, the most important concept for young readers to grasp about literary fictions is that of narrative point of view, through which subject positions are constructed and ideological assumptions inscribed. Further, narrative discourses are not just agents of representation but also objects of representation. The interaction of discourse types within narrative allows them to disclose their own narrative processes, hence permitting evaluation of the subject positions they imply.

Readers can identify not only the same 'story' in a book but also a common 'significance', though this will not necessarily mean that either the same subject position or the same ideological frame has been invoked. Readers may still actively engage with a text by constructing a subject position from within their everyday social practice in order to oppose the position implied by the text. Texts can, however, firmly construct particular subject positions through the processes of focalization and inference-making.

Focalization is particularly important to any consideration of subjectivity or ideology. Unqualified identification with focalizers attributes a coherent reality and objectivity to the world constructed by the text, and in doing so constructs a false subjectivity and a self-hood which is only mimetic of the focalizing selfhood in the text. Identification with focalizers is one of the chief methods by which a text socializes its readers, as they efface their own selfhood and internalize the perceptions and attitudes of the focalizer and are thus reconstituted as subjects within the text. The process of inference-making is a similarly inexplicit aspect of how a reader, moving around amongst discourse, story and significance, may become implicated in a specific subject position. Inferences themselves are broadly of two kinds, those that bear on story and those that bear on significance. But the two are not always separable, and by becoming implicated in story, readers may become implicated in significance.

On the other hand, various kinds of distancing or estranging strategies encourage the constitution of a reading self in interaction with the other constituted in and by the text. Within a fuller dialectic, therefore, readers will be engaging with a structured form of the larger intersubjective process whereby the self negotiates its own coming into being in relation to society. A text which does not demand specific world knowledge or particular presuppositions, or insists on an indeterminacy of such knowledge, can be said to refuse both a single implied reader and a simple identifiable subject position from which a real reader might engage with the text. Meaningfulness gives way to playfulness, from which new meanings might arise.

This chapter has discussed or alluded to several strategies by which readers may be prevented from singular identification with a focalizer, and so prevented from adopting a singular subject position. Strategies of major significance not discussed are certain kinds of intertextual reference and carnivalesque, interrogative textuality. These will be the topics of the next two chapters. First, Chapter 3 will be concerned with intertextual allusiveness, which may indicate the presence of more than one interpretative frame and require top-down reading of some sophistication.

TAKING IT FURTHER

Most of the work on the relationship between focalization and subjectivity in fiction, and its effect on the transaction between readers and texts, still remains to be done. It is, I think, one of the most important areas to be developed in the criticism not only of children's fiction but of fiction in general. This present chapter is a beginning, and I will return to the topic continually throughout the rest of the book, but there is much more to be done both with the genres I will be concerned with and with other genres. The area is crucial to readings of realist texts intended for young adult readers.

Chapter 4 will take up the question of interrogative texts, but more generally texts which offer what I have here called estranged subject positions need to be explored and their reading encouraged. Particular areas which ought to be developed far beyond what I have had space for here are: shifts in focalizer; focalizers with whom reader identification is discouraged; multi-stranded narration; and metafiction.

Finally, ideological issues of race, class and gender – of multiculturalism and children's literature in its broadest sense – need to be discussed much more in terms of representation than has been the practice to date. The old theme-and-content analysis serves these areas very poorly, though the dominant practice amongst children's authors of employing a single focalizer is a continuing barrier to representing the *other* as anything but object (see Stephens, 1990b).

Mayne's *Drift*, discussed in Chapter 1, might be considered again in this context, since it constructs its concern with race contact through dual focalization. A useful comparison might be made between Needle's *My Mate Shofiq* and Leeson's *The Third Class Genie*, and then further comparison with books by African American writers which are focalized through black characters. Virginia Hamilton's *Arilla Sun Down*, for example, is a remarkable exploration of identity and subjectivity. Hamilton's *Dustlands* trilogy (1980) is also of considerable interest as a reworking of the 'high fantasy' genre with black protagonists. A convenient resource for details of American multicultural books is Cullinan (1989, pp. 575–620).

In general, questions such as the following can be asked of apparently culturally diverse books: are cultures and experiences which are not those of a white middle class represented as inferior or ineffectual; do characters demonstrate subjectivity, or are they objects or even caricatures; does the book's language implicitly assume the superiority of a form of 'standard' English; and do illustrations adequately represent distinctive physical features, and avoid cultural stereotypes?

FURTHER READING

The relationship between ideology and subjectivity is complex and hotly debated. Subjectivity has long been a focal point for disputation between Marxism and humanism: for a comprehensive discussion, see Paul Smith (1988). For extended, opposing arguments about the status of subjectivity within the Marxist intellectual tradition, see Ellis (1976) and the reply by Molina (1977).

For fiction and multiculturalism see Banfield (1978), Greenfield (1986), St Clair (1988) and Stephens (1990b). On the theory of focalization, see Rimmon-Kenan (1983, pp. 71–85).

THREE

Not by words alone: language, intertextuality, society

During the transmission of a text, author and audience can be said to share a field of discourse through the author's representation of phenomena, objects, events, etc., and the audience's decoding or (re-)construction of those representations. Such a process of decoding depends upon the audience's semiotic and literary competency, especially in terms of a knowledge of conventions and genres and often of a memory of other books similar or related in genre, theme, or story. The production of meaning from the interrelationships between audience, text, other texts, and the socio-cultural determinations of significance, is a process which may be conveniently summed up in the term *intertextuality*. Further, no text exists in isolation from other texts, and from their conventions and genres. In the sense, then, that all texts inhabit an intertextual space, intertextuality is analogous to the intersubjectivity which human individuals experience in their day-to-day existence and which gives shape and purpose to individual subjectivity. As might therefore be expected, intersubjectivity is often constituted as an overt theme in texts which foreground their own intertextuality.

THE FOCUSED TEXT AND ITS INTERTEXTS

There may be several kinds of relationship between a *focused text*, that is, the text which is the immediate object of attention (Miller 1985, p. 21) and other texts. The focused text may stand in some kind of relationship to:

(a) specific earlier texts (or *pre-texts*) which are obviously alluded to by direct quotation or by allusion – some retellings of fairy stories, biblical stories, or myths may have such clear pretextual relationships;

(b) a well-known story existing in a number of versions, none of which is specifically identifiable – an extended example is Fiona French's *Snow White in New York* (discussed below), which is obviously intertextual without needing a specific pre-text;

(c) an archetype, such as the quest, the lone survivor, the earthly paradise, the waste land, the wandering hero who frees the land of a curse or monster, the lost child, the despised younger brother who achieves greatness, etc.;

(d) genres and conventions – folktales and the 'school story' are examples of quite different genres which both, to a large extent, are conventionalized in their contents, structures, characters and patterns of represented behaviour;

(e) socio-historical narratives or moments – for example, citation of such documents as the Gettysburg address in Madeleine L'Engle's *A Wrinkle in Time* makes a major contribution to the mid-twentieth-century Cold War ideology pervading that book and becoming constituted as its theme;

(f) other discourses, such as painting, popular song, film, television and, in recent times, even advertisements – the picture books of Maurice Sendak are excellent examples of such intertextualities (see especially the fascinating discussion of *Outside Over There* in Cott 1983, pp. 68–84, which documents the ultimate pre-text, in the Grimm tale 'The Juniper Tree', and a remarkable range of intertexts including Sendak's earlier books, Mozart's *The Magic Flute*, Runge's painting *The Hulsenbeck Children*, William Blake's paintings, and Mahler's *The Youth's Magic Horn*);

(g) subsequent texts: recent writers on intertextuality (especially Riffaterre 1980a, 1980b, 1981) maintain that its operation is achronological. This is an important consideration for children's literature, for two reasons. Children (like adults) are very likely to encounter texts in a fairly random order, and, more importantly, children will have encountered many texts before developing a sufficiently sophisticated sense of time to be able to organize cultural artefacts into a meaningful order.

The processes of intertextuality are a special problem with children's books. On the one hand, there can be no presumption that the audience has been previously exposed to specific pre-texts or conventions of narrative; on the other hand, however, because intertextuality is a strategy whereby a text relates to existing discourses and achieves intelligibility, it often plays a major part in attempts to produce determinable meanings and to acculturate the audience. It does this whenever ideas and attitudes towards these ideas are placed within a particular discourse, as, for example, when constructions of femaleness are situated within the 'school story' genre.

DISCOURSES FUNCTIONING AS INTERTEXTS

The literature written for children is also radically intertextual because it has no special discourse of its own. While the literature is subject to some constraints on certain kinds of linguistic complexity (in syntax, lexis and figurative language), and certain register choices which occur in poorer quality writing can impart a precious and affected quality, these features aren't enough to constitute a distinctive discourse. Rather, writing for children exists at the intersection of a number of other discourses, and illustrates acutely the extent to which language is both a semiotic system and a product of its own history. The discourses of particular importance to texts written for children fall into three groups:

(1) Traditional narrative forms and genres, such as folktale, romance, and naturalism (or 'realism').
(2) Specialized contents, which overlap with the preceding category but also include such materials as mythology (particularly classical, Scandinavian and Celtic, but with some attention to North American, Australian and African aboriginal 'mythologies'), biblical story, and certain favoured historical periods (especially the Middle Ages, with special reference to the Arthurian legends; the nineteenth century; and, in more recent literature, the mid-twentieth century).
(3) A variety of discourses drawn upon by fiction as part of the process of constructing a discourse for fiction, and which bring with them ideologies bearing on social purpose and structure. The function and effect of these other discourses is to articulate the orientation of the embedding discourse. They operate quite obviously, as, for example, with religion, ethics, humanism and cultural materialism. One example can be seen in the mid-twen-

tieth-century humanist discourse which pervades Lloyd Alexander's *Chronicles of Prydain* (particularly evident, say, in Chapters 18 and 19 of *Taran Wanderer*); an example of a different kind
is the parodic and satiric uses of the discourses of 'Government'
in Jan Needle's *The Size Spies*. Such discourses may also be more
implicit and function more covertly to articulate an attitude, as
with notions of 'other' societies discernible in the discourses of
medievalism and orientalism. In Susan Cooper's 'The Dark is
Rising' sequence actions in present time are invested with significance because of the moral values discerned in England's past
time and mediated through concepts such as 'the gift of grama-
rye' (p. 107). At the same time, however, such a process tends to
invest the past with more value than the present, usually doing
so implicitly, but occasionally making the position explicit, as
when in the episode of Will Stanton and the witch Maggie the
contemporary name for the track Will is standing on, 'Tramp's
Alley', is contemptuously dismissed by Merriman: 'Look hard
at this road, boy, and do not call it by vulgar names again' (p.
75). Contemporary social discourse is in this way belittled at the
expense of a discourse constructed as a replication of past discourses.

A specific text will be grounded in a particular discourse from
group one or two, but it will tend also to be influenced by one or
both of the other groups. For example, the discourses of group three
are crucial for any consideration of the socializing and acculturaling
effects of children's literature, since their goal (explicit or not) is to
mediate between the elements of groups one and two and the
reader, in order to determine the nature of the reader's reception of
the text. It is in this context that intertextuality is exploited to inculcate knowledge about contemporary culture and to illustrate how
that knowledge is to be used. The discourse of children's literature
is thus in essence, and often self-consciously, intertextual in all of
the current senses of this term.

It is not my intention in this chapter to attempt to examine all the
intertextual situations that are possible, but I will discuss some
examples of major types, beginning with perhaps the most obvious,
the explicit presence of pre-texts in the retelling of known stories,
such as the folk (or 'fairy') stories of the Grimms or Perrault. Such
retellings can function in two different ways.

First, the 'original' story may be naturalized within the idioms and cultural codes contemporary with the retelling. Disney versions of such stories are a notorious example of how contemporary values and aspirations may be encoded through the remaking of old stories. These versions are often not intertextual in effect because their dissemination is so widespread and general that young audiences are exposed to no other variant. This situation is a clear example of the problem with the notion of intertextuality referred to above; that is, that for any book children encounter, the availability of pre-texts and intertexts is rather random. They are likely to have been exposed to related texts only for some books, and then at varying stages in any individual's reading experience. Second, the retelling might be consciously played off against some common notion of the shape and content of an 'original' text, and might hence assume that the audience will be in a position to weigh one against the other. In such a case, because of the coexistence within the one discourse space of pre-text and focused text the significance of the story will tend to be situated not in the focused text but in the process of interaction between the texts. That is, the effect is intertextual in its fullest sense.

ROALD DAHL'S *REVOLTING RHYMES*: INTERTEXTUAL ICONOCLASM

The climax of Dahl's re-version of 'Little Red Riding Hood and the Wolf' (1984) exemplifies these aspects of intertextuality especially clearly, and effectively draws attention to what it is doing through the way the doggerel couplets used to tell the story are interrupted in order to embed quotations from a more conventional version (the pre-text), and then this embedded material is itself unconventionally refashioned. By quoting the most consistent feature of the Red Riding Hood story, the question-and-answer dialogue between girl and wolf, Dahl signals that he is working within a chronology of versions and expects his audience to be familiar with the features of the conventional story:

> In came the little girl in red.
> She stopped. She stared. And then she said,

> *'What great big ears you have, Grandma.'*
> *'All the better to hear you with,'* the Wolf replied.

'What great big eyes you have, Grandma,'
said Little Red Riding Hood.
'All the better to see you with,' the Wolf replied.

Wolf attempting to restore conventional story.

He sat there watching her and smiled.
He thought, I'm going to eat this child.
Compared with her old Grandmamma
She's going to taste like caviare.

Then Little Red Riding Hood said, 'But Grandma,
what a lovely great big furry coat you have on.'
'That's wrong!' cried Wolf. 'Have you forgot
'To tell me what BIG TEETH I've got?
'Ah well, no matter what you say,
'I'm going to eat you anyway.'
The small girl smiles. One eyelid flickers.
She whips a pistol from her knickers.
She aims it at the creature's head
And *bang bang bang*, she shoots him dead.

(Dahl, *Revolting Rhymes*, pp. 38–9)

The generally iconoclastic narration of the well-known story alerts the audience for some surprise element, though this need not necessarily be a positive outcome for Red Riding Hood (in the immediately preceding story, after all, the Three Bears ate Goldilocks). The shifting between the two modes of story-telling creates a playful suspense, and the Wolf's attempt to restore the 'proper' version (an obvious accenting of how improper Dahl's version is) foregrounds the outrageousness of the re-vision of the story that immediately follows. So far, any child familiar with a conventional version easily follows the game.

The intertextuality becomes more problematic with, firstly, the changed ending and its accompanying generic shift (into, roughly, the style of a Western double-cross), and then with the effects of *knickers*. There is a hint of taboo about the mention of an undergarment and Red Riding Hood's placing of her hand inside it, and these effects are accessible to a child. But *knickers* has a variable signification, depending on the assumptions drawn from context and register: it can be used merely descriptively; it can function as a mild swear-word; and television usage (principally in situation comedy) marks it as a mild, mock-taboo word, something that gets a laugh but doesn't really shock (At the end of the 1980s the word's associations were still marginally respectable. For example, a brand of panty could be named *No Knickers*, but television advertisements promoting the product noticeably exploited teasing, 'naughtiness' and exposure). The semantic range and cultural coding involved in this word are beyond the reach of the majority of the book's juvenile audience. Less accessible still is the comment Red Riding Hood's action makes on those aspects of the story which deal with seduction and female submissiveness (Bettelheim 1976, pp. 166–83; Zipes 1983, pp. 29–31) – a gun in the knickers is a fairly clear symbol of female self-assertive sexuality (though Red Riding Hood is still feminine enough to turn what's left of the wolf into a fur coat).

FOREGROUNDING THE INTERTEXT

An interesting comparison can be made between Dahl's version and the series of exchanges between the young woman and the wolf in Catherine Storr's *Clever Polly and the Stupid Wolf* (1955, reprinted 1967), where in several of the stories the wolf attempts to capture Polly by trying to impose a fairy-story sequence on events, and is thwarted when Polly either breaches narrative cohesion, or pushes the sequence to a logical conclusion unfavourable to the wolf, or because fairy story incidents prove impractical in the 'real' world. As with the Dahl, these strategies dramatize aspects of representation, narration, and art–life relationships.

One of Storr's main interests in these stories is in semantic slippage and the arbitrary linking of signifiers to signified phenomena, conditions or events, and she exploits the transactions between text and pre-text to bring out the importance of these aspects of language to social interaction. In contrast to Polly, the wolf is a subject controlled by his social role, that is, by his role as a fairy-tale wolf whose major function is to attempt to eat little girls. Key parts of this control are his entrapment by convention and by language itself. The title of the fourth story, 'Little Polly Riding Hood', immediately offers its readers access to the game of sameness and difference. And when Polly meets the wolf on the way to her grandmother's house, readers are reminded not only that the pre-text itself exists in very different versions (the wolf is sure that 'mine is the true story, and yours is just invented'), but also that changing social circumstances redefine and restructure significance. The wolf, the conventional embodiment of threat and power, has become the subordinate speaker in the following unequal encounter:

> 'Where does your grandmother live, Polly Riding Hood?'
> 'Over the other side of the town,' answered Polly.
> The wolf frowned.
> 'It ought to be "Through the wood",' he said. 'But perhaps town will do. How do you get there, Polly Riding Hood?'
> 'First I take a train and then I take a bus,' said Polly.
> The wolf stamped his foot.
> 'No, no, no, no!' he shouted. 'That's all wrong. You can't say that. You've got to say, "By that path winding through the trees", or something like that. You can't go by trains and buses and things. It isn't fair.'
> 'Well, I could say that', said Polly, 'but it wouldn't be true. I do have to go by bus and train to see my grandma, so what's the good of saying I don't?'
>
> (Storr, *Clever Polly and the Stupid Wolf*, p. 18)

The existence of the pre-text affects not only Polly's answer but also the wolf's question, by giving it the force of a loaded question. Because the answer *un-loads* the question, the questioner's status is shifted from dominant to subordinate speaker, and his subsequent corrective and concessive ('ought to be', 'perhaps . . . will do') only emphasize his subordination. The next exchange repeats the process, moving through the questioner's increasing frustration to culminate now in the contrast between his notion of some formula which approximates to his expectation and the assertion of a simple principle of truth-value which conditions the answer he receives. The wolf's inability to assimilate the re-encoding of the expected conversation becomes a measure of his impotence.

Text and pre-text interact differently in another story, 'Monday's Child', in which Polly and the wolf argue about the relative merits of their versions of the well-known rhyme 'Monday's child is fair of face', and this leads to a discussion on the uses of literature. Here, the existence of radically different versions of the same text problematizes Polly's version, by focusing awareness on the arbitrariness of the act which links traits and fortunes to the day of the week on which a person is born. The first two lines of the wolf-lore version,

> Monday's child is fairly tough
> Tuesday's child is tender enough,

underline how such formulas arise out of simple oppositions, and then the semantically weak rhyme-word, 'enough' (which is further thinned because it repeats the earlier qualifier, 'fairly') plays on the arbitrariness of the form. On a broader level, the debate mirrors the larger intertextual game engaged in by the whole book, and while the wolf concludes that 'literary discussions . . . often don't get one anywhere' (p. 49), the story still points to the book's major theme, that knowing society's codes, especially its cultural and linguistic codes, and knowing how to manipulate them, means power.

CHILDREN'S ICONOCLASM AND USES OF INTERTEXTUALITY

The relationship between children's literature and contemporary cultural discourses – social and linguistic conventions, oral traditions, and so on – is an important aspect of its intertextuality. This is a complex relationship, especially in the extent to which the literature implicitly reflects a culture's dominant ideologies, or is sometimes a vehicle for acculturating its audience, or sometimes seeks to parody or subvert one or other of those ideologies. It may perform two or more of these functions simultaneously. Consider the following joke:

'Why did the computer cross the road?'
'Because it was programmed by a chicken.'

This variation on an old stock joke serves as an obvious reminder that meaning is not the product of some closed linguistic system, but emerges as part of a complex interconnection of language, society, and a variety of discourses, some oral, some written. The comedy of the joke arises essentially from a threefold process. Firstly, there is a presumption that the audience is familiar with the sub-genre of joke that is being alluded to, and so both recognizes the key pre-text, 'Why did the chicken cross the road?', and expects the usual sort of anti-climactic answer. Secondly, the genre is simultaneously made strange and modernized by the substitution of 'computer' for 'chicken', while the audience's knowledge of the pretext maintains a trace of the original 'chicken' in the first line inasmuch as 'computer' also signifies 'not-chicken'. The substitution in turn sets up the third process, which produces the anticlimax: this derives in part from a simple verbal structure, from the delayed occurrence of the displaced term 'chicken', and in part from the less specific pre-text of social awareness, the knowledge that chickens do not program computers.

Jokes of this kind, which children invent and tell to one another, are an index of an early fascination with notions of intertextuality. This often takes the form of parody or travesty of the pre-text, and its purpose often seems to be iconoclastic, perhaps as an attempt to subvert what is perceived as the dominant discourse – the discourse of parents and teachers with its expectations about propriety and its perceived hostility towards certain taboo words and subjects. Hence a lot of playground rhymes seem to be making fun of authority, or else they deal more or less directly with the taboo areas of sexuality and excretion. Interestingly, the existence of the pre-text also enables quite comic disappointments of expectation, as in the computer-and-chicken joke, which are, in potential at least, a training ground for a more advanced handling of linguistic, social and literary discourses.

A good example of this play with language and with literary and social intertexts is the enormous number of existing parodies of 'Mary had a little lamb' (there are thirteen recorded in *Cinderella Dressed in Yella*, pp. 120–1, and the editors note that the variations are too numerous for them to list). Some of the variants are mainly a reaction against the 'niceness' of the language and situation of the original, as in the selection of events and register of the following:

> Mary had a little lamb,
> Her father shot it dead,
> And now it goes to school with her
> Between two hunks of bread.

A degree of linguistic sophistication enters these texts when they explore the polysemous signification of 'had', making use of its capacity also to signify 'give birth to' or 'eat'. One such piece which toys with some taboo areas of sexuality proceeds by introducing a variation into the first line ('sheep' for 'lamb'), by breaking the rhyme scheme, and then working back to the original words but with a different signification:

> Mary had a little sheep,
> And with that sheep she went to sleep.
> The sheep turned out to be a ram
> And Mary had a little lamb.

A more complicated question with this piece is that of the social ideology implicit within it, as its witty travesty replaces the pre-text's construction of woman as feminine, innocent and clean, with a more overt anti-feminism which presents woman as simultaneously a sex object and sexually ignorant. Thus the attempt to subvert a particular social ideology is actually preconditioned and controlled by an attitude which is only a darker aspect of that very ideology's construction of woman. Indeed, the text's playfulness only thinly masks a hostile anti-feminism. This rhyme is a simple example, but well illustrates the attitudinal complexity that results when different modes of intertextualty intersect within a single textual site.

These rhymes are multiple re-encodings of a familiar pre-text. Other ways in which discourse may differently encode the one 'story' are clearly seen in versions of traditional fairy tales. I will illustrate this from two versions of the *Snow White* story, and three texts which are retellings of Perrault's *Cinderella*.

RETELLING THE 'STORY': (A) TWO VERSIONS OF *SNOW WHITE*

The two versions of *Snow White* have been chosen for their obvious differences. The first, from *Hilda Boswell's Best Book of Fairy Tales*, represents a common post-Disney version of the tale. It is an inexpensive 'supermarket' book, cheaply produced, on rather coarse paper, with well drawn and neatly printed line-and-pastel illustrations appearing on every page. The characters appear in costumes which are the kind of ersatz medieval-to-eighteenth-century dress which is the staple of such books. The first story in this particular volume, *Rapunzel*, at one point nicely indicates the origins of the illustrations when the blinded prince is represented in a pose and with a hair-style and lower facial features borrowed directly from Pre-Raphaelite painting.

The second book, costing about six times as much, is Fiona French's picture book *Snow White in New York* (1986). The verbal text here has been reduced to only 400 words, quite brief even for a picture book, and the pictures themselves are more central to the narrative than are Boswell's illustrations. French begins with the conventional 'Once upon a time' opening, but the story is set in

1930 New York high society and major variations occur with both events and characters: for example, Snow White's period of banishment is spent as a singer with a seven-piece jazz group, and her marriage at the end is to a newspaper reporter, not a prince. The book's production is also distinctive: the colours of the pictures are luminous, and the visual intertexts range from a basis in art deco, as established especially by the title page, through Charles Keeping's drawing style (especially in the cross-hatching used in depicting city sky-lines), to pop art, to Picasso's blue period. The costumes and settings are appropriate for New York high society of the 1920s and 1930s.

The differences between the versions are immediately apparent, so I will illustrate these from their respective openings:

(1) Boswell
Once upon a time in a far-away land there lived a pretty little princess called Snow White. She had skin as white as snow, hair as black as ebony and lips as red as cherries.
Her mother the Queen had died when she was quite young and some time afterward her father, the King, married another wife and brought her to the palace. The new Queen was very beautiful but she was so proud and haughty that she could not bear anyone to be prettier that herself. She owned a wonderful, magic mirror . . .

(2) French
Once upon a time in New York there was a poor little rich girl called Snow White. Her mother was dead and for a while she lived happily with her father. But one day he married again . . .

All the papers said that Snow White's stepmother was the classiest dame in New York. But no one knew that she was the Queen of the Underworld. She liked to see herself in the New York Mirror.

(Two Versions of *Snow White*)

Both versions abbreviate the opening by following the Disney tradition of omitting all but a passing mention of Snow White's mother. This omission has consequences for the physical description of Snow White, since in the early versions the attributes of her beauty derive from the mother's visual linking of snow, blood, and ebony window-frame. The Boswell version is a pastiche of some earlier retellings, but by retaining 'ebony', even though it will have little meaning for most children, and substituting 'cherries' for the blood, it exists in an awkward relationship to the earliest pre-texts, neither shedding them nor evoking them. In contrast, French makes no mention of Snow White's appearance, and when she and her step-mother appear on adjacent pages (viii–ix) French uses instead a more conventional iconography: Snow White is blonde with big blue eyes, the stepmother dark with narrow green eyes. Further, French's open-ing three sentences overtly manipulate intertextuality. On the one hand, she has pared the usual details of the Snow White story back to a bare outline, and on the other, she has evoked fresh intertexts in the literature of and about 1930s America. The most obvious change in the opening is the recontextualizing of 'little' from a fairy-story cliché to a modern socio-cultural cliché in 'a poor little rich girl'. Secondly, she tightens up the relationship between change and me-nace by means of the temporal cohesion of the second and third sentences: 'for a while she lived happily . . . But one day . . .'.

Boswell's pastiche employs, especially in its first couple of pages, the 'precious' register I mentioned at the beginning of this chapter, which pervades much children's literature. This doesn't include the opening vagueness of time and place, which is common in folk tale (it is French who is obviously deviant in locating the well-known tale in New York), but is apparent in the penchant for semantically thin diminutives, as in 'pretty little princess'. It is partly a social convention that young girls are 'pretty' where mature women, like the new Queen, are 'beautiful', and the thought of some one 'pret-tier' than her which threatens the Queen anticipates Snow White's growing into that role. By the bottom of the first page this change has happened, with Snow White 'growing prettier and prettier as each day passed'. Some form of 'pretty' has thus appeared four times within a dozen lines of narrative. The use of such semantically slight epithets is also evidenced by 'wonderful'.

A second aspect of this register is a set of terms and idioms used for making the discourse strange, and the two versions make a very interesting comparison in this regard. Boswell draws on a set which consists of elevated, slightly archaic terms and phrases not normally used in contemporary speech. An example in the cited extract is the second term of the doublet 'proud and haughty'. Other examples occurring soon after (they tend to cluster at the beginning of stories) are, 'resolved in her heart' and 'unwilling to do this cruel deed'. French makes strange the story by narrating and illustrating it in the idioms of other discourses, and the comic discrepancies between the chosen and traditional discourses emphasize the strangeness.

Such touches as the apparent move towards realism in the joke by which the stepmother's mirror is converted into a newspaper interact closely with the illustrations. In this particular example, the change is strongly enforced by the accompanying illustration of overlaid front-page stories. The special language used to articulate the story into the 1930s setting, with idioms such as 'classiest dame', is, of course, as archaic for contemporary speech as anything in Boswell, but is far more powerful in effect, contributing both to the comedy and to a sense that an archetype of jealousy and struggle may both be realized in discourses of very different kinds and modified by social conditions of time and place.

RETELLING THE 'STORY': (B) THREE VERSIONS OF *CINDERELLA*

The three versions of *Cinderella* are by Arthur Quiller-Couch (1910), John Fowles (1974) and Angela Carter (1982). All three are part-translation, part-adaptation, and derive from Perrault without any mediating texts. But since they are as much adaptation as translation, what they chiefly illustrate as a group is not so much the relationship between text and pre-text as the relationship between texts and aspects of the social discourses of the culture which produced them. Even where one of the versions follows the Perrault closely, this becomes unimportant because of shifts in culture and semantics. An examination of the three versions thus offers insight into the ways texts articulate ideologies (for a useful account of general principles, see Sutherland 1985).

In general, Quiller-Couch (Q) cultivates an antique, eighteenth-century ethos for the story. The collection in which it appears was illustrated by Edmund Dulac, and his decision to depict eighteenth century dress was defended by Quiller-Couch with the argument that the literature itself was then 'at the acme of its vogue' (*Preface*, p. vii), and Dulac represents the costumes very well. Quiller-Couch himself retains and augments details which promote this ethos. At the other extreme, Fowles (F) deletes such material and tries to imply modernity. While Quiller-Couch and Fowles offer an obvious contrast between the Edwardian and the Modern, Fowles makes heavy use of a nakedly didactic discourse, whereas Quiller-Couch's pursuit of the same moral objectives – that is, models of exemplary behaviour – is somewhat masked by his concern with historical period and proper detail. Fowles directly advocates good conduct and deplores the bad; but Carter leans more towards indirect commentary on behaviour through the cultivation of irony. To illustrate these differences, I will once again focus on a small section, namely the invitation to and the preparations for the first ball (Quiller-Couch (Q), pp. 50–3; Fowles (F), pp. 7–8; Carter (C), pp. 104–5). All quotations will be followed by the Perrault original.

The attitudes of each writer as represented in their accounts of the invitation diverge considerably:

[a] It happened that the King's son gave a ball, and sent invitations through the kingdom to every person of quality. Our two misses were invited among the rest, for they cut a great figure in that part of the country. (Q, p. 50)

[b] It happened about this time that the King's son decided to give a Great Ball, to which he asked everyone of importance. The two proud sisters were invited, because they showed off everywhere they went and stupid people took them for what they seemed. (F, p. 7)

[c] The king's son decided to hold a ball to which he invited all the aristocracy. Our two young ladies received their invitations, for they were well connected. (C, p. 104)

[d] Il arriva que le fils du Roi donna un bal, et qu'il en pria toutes les personnes de qualité: nos deux Demoiselles en furent aussi priées, car elles faisaient grande figure dans le Pays. (P, p. 172)

    (Quiller-Couch, Fowles, Carter, Perrault, four versions of Cinderella)

There are three key details here. Firstly, the recipients of the invitation. Q, in keeping with both his pro-upper class feelings and his attempt to impart an antique atmosphere to the story, follows Perrault's 'les personnes de qualité' with the phrase, already long since archaic in English, 'person of quality', which combines the senses of F's vaguely qualitative 'everyone of importance' and C's simple class-designator 'all the aristocracy' (the most accurate as a translation of Perrault).

Secondly, the end of each extract defines how the sisters qualify for the invitation. F's heavy-handed pointing of the moral judgements is very clear here, in the series 'proud . . . showed off . . . stupid . . . what they seemed'. Q suggests irony by the qualification 'in that part of the country', while C's 'for they were well connected' is the subtlest irony of all, playing on the reader's knowledge of the story (Cinderella's godmother proves to be a much more useful connection, and by the end of the story Cinderella will have achieved the ultimate in connection), and looking forward to the more socially cynical of Perrault's two morals (that talent is useless unless its possessor is well connected).

Thirdly, there is the designation of the two sisters which functions as a narratorial comment on their social position: they are 'our two misses' (Q), 'our two young ladies' (C), and 'the two proud sisters' (F): F has selected a descriptor which overtly states a moral judgement, while Q and C have exploited the strategy of narrator-narratee collusion by picking up the first person plural pronoun *our* from Perrault and then deploying it in such a way as to evoke an ironical use of current modes of reference. The terms recur in a later conversation:

[e]   Whilst she was dressing them one asked her: 'Cinderella, would you not like to be going to the ball?'
      'Alas! miss,' said Cinderella, 'you are making fun of me. It is not for the like of me to be there.'
      'You are right, girl. Folks would laugh indeed to see *Cinder-slut* at a ball!' (Q, p. 53)

[f]   Then she very kindly offered to do their hair herself. But as she did it, they made fun of her.
      'Don't you wish *you* were going to the ball, Cinderella?'
      'You know it's not my place,' she said. 'I think you're being very cruel.'
      'It certainly isn't your place. People would die laughing if they saw an Ash-blanket dancing.' (F, p. 8)

[g]   As she was combing their hair, they said to her:
      'Cindrella, dear, wouldn't you like to go to the ball yourself?'
      'Oh, don't make fun of me, my ladies, how could I possibly go to the ball!'
      'Quite right, too; everyone would laugh themselves silly to see Cinder-britches at a ball.' (C, p. 105)

[h]   En les coiffant, elles lui disaient: <<Cendrillon, serais-tu bien aisé d'aller au Bal? – Hélas, Mesdemoiselles, vous vous moquez de moi, ce n'est pas là ce qu'il me faut. – Tu as raison, on rirait bien si on voyait un Cucendron aller au Bal.>> (P, p. 172)
      (Quiller-Couch, Fowles, Carter, Perrault, four versions of *Cinderella*)

By now it is clear how heavily F is directing reader response: not only does Cinderella make her offer 'very kindly', but the vindictiveness of the teasing is made more obvious: first, Cinderella's rejoinder to the stepsisters' teasing has been converted into the narrator's description of the teasing, and then she is given a more remonstrative rejoinder which is, in effect, a spelling out of the motive behind the teasing. Finally, the stepsisters' vindictiveness is further stressed by the cohesive repetition in 'isn't your place'.

The other versions generate some subtlety through the manipulation of vocatives: those used by Cinderella are appropriate modes of address for a servant – 'miss' in Q, which is underlined by the responding vocative 'girl' (a normal address to a servant), and 'my ladies' in C. But in each the address is double-edged for the audience because of the ironical use shortly before. C gives an extra nudge to the effect by the sisters' vocative, 'Cindrella, dear'.

All three versions depart quite drastically from Perrault's account of Cinderella's possible response to this treatment. In doing so, each further exemplifies the kind of language use I have been pointing to, though now the irony of Q, who greatly expands this motif, is replaced by a much more judgemental tone:

[i]   Anyone but Cinderella would have pinned on their mob-caps
      awry; and if you or I had been in her place, I won't swear but that
      we might have pushed in the pins just a trifle carelessly. But she
      had no malice in her nature; she attired them to perfection, though
      they found fault with her all the while it was doing, and quite for-
      got to thank her when it was done. (Q, p. 53)
[j]   A girl less sweet-natured than Cinderella would have paid them
      out by doing their hair all wrong. But she actually did it very well.
      (F, p. 8)
[k]   Any other girl but Cinderella would have made horrid tangles of
      their hair after that, out of spite; but she was kind, and resisted the
      temptation. (C, p. 105)
[l]   Une autre que Cendrillon les aurait coiffées de travers; mais elle
      était bonne, et elle les coiffa parfaitement bien. (P, p. 172)
      (Quiller-Couch, Fowles, Carter, Perrault, four versions of *Cinderella*)

At this point, Q's advocacy of good conduct becomes blatant. Cinderella becomes the epitome of patient endurance and innate goodness, and the narrator-narratee transaction is used to raise and set aside what is imagined to be the normal reader response: the reader can approve of Cinderella's surpassing virtue or be convicted of thinking and feeling like a carping, ungrateful stepsister. (It is likely, as well, that Q's text here incidentally incorporates some advice to contemporary servants; the revenge imagined represents a

cunning form of pay-back, rather than the obvious, and impossible
to get away with, suggestions in the later texts.) Fowles likewise advocates 'sweet-natured' behaviour in the face of reader response,
here represented more covertly by the colloquialisms 'paid them
out' and 'doing . . . all wrong'. Carter is alone in endowing the
character with a complex emotion. Cinderella *is* tempted to act
spitefully and vengefully, but her innate kindness wins out. While
this representation still assents to the pre-text's model of remarkably good behaviour, Carter's method does communicate to her
readers the insight that true virtue is a question of choice, not of re-
flex, and makes the best of a rather morally repressive story.

INTERTEXTUALITIES OF THEME AND ALLUSION

To illustrate some of the complexities of intertextuality in stories not
obviously based on traditional material, I will include here some
discussion of two books which make an interesting pair, *The Pirate
Uncle*, a book for younger readers (middle primary) by the New
Zealand writer Margaret Mahy, and *Handles*, a book for a slightly
older age group by the English writer Jan Mark. Each of these books
makes much internal use of obligatory intertextuality, but as a pair
they are intertextually related to one another in an accidental way,
and thus demonstrate how intertextuality functions in the large
sense of a cultural discourse – in this case, humanistic children's
novels, written on opposite sides of the world in English, dealing
with a particular thematic complex. The two books are similar, then,
in that they are concerned with essentially the same theme, they
both explore the relationships between language, signs and culture,
and both are concerned with name-bestowing and selfhood. More
obviously, both are framed by the conventional situation whereby
their child characters are temporarily relocated in the house of a
little-known relative, where they must explore and come to terms
with a new context and situation. Displacement or relocation are
common strategies in children's fiction by which main characters
are forced to come to terms with their own subjectivity through a
new context of intersubjective relations. The shift also foregrounds
that aspect of the reading process whereby readers are enabled to
try out subject positions different from those within which they
usually function.

The opening paragraph of *The Pirate Uncle* clearly signals the nature of the book's intertextuality:

> Nicholas Battle, nine years old, thin, fair and thoughtful, was sitting behind the chair in the corner of the sitting- room reading a really good book. It was about two children who had been sent to stay with a mysterious uncle who lived in Cornwall, England. (A lot of good stories begin like this.) Nick hadn't got very far in the story yet, but already he was pretty sure that the uncle was a smuggler and possibly a highwayman too. What he did not know was that a coincidence was about to happen.
>
> (Mahy, *The Pirate Uncle*, p. 9)

What appears to be a simple paragraph is in fact a remarkably complex opening to a light-hearted, comic novel which not only entertains its readers but also unobtrusively takes them on a tour of intertextual space. The opening flaunts the novel's conventions. Nicholas, who is to be one of the main characters, is introduced as a stereotypical bookworm, though the epithets describing him – 'thin, fair and thoughtful' – jostle teasingly against his surname. The mid-paragraph parenthesis suggests that the book Nicholas is reading is generically identifiable, though the real reader is unlikely to have seen many examples, and will almost certainly be too young to have read such specific intertexts as, for instance, Susan Cooper's *Over Sea, Under Stone*, perhaps the best-known book about children 'who had been sent to stay with a mysterious uncle who lived in Cornwall, England'. The point, I think, is that Mahy is constructing a concept of genre and consequent expectation. If, or when, readers subsequently read *Over Sea, Under Stone* it will be intertextually modified by the experience of reading *The Pirate Uncle*, even though the two books have nothing else in common, and *Over Sea, Under Stone* is the earlier book by a decade.

Having established a generic context, Mahy introduces next the readerly habit of hypothesizing about the future course of a narrative, and then an old standby and problematic of fiction, coincidence. Here, however, the focus is on coincidence between 'life' and 'art', and opens the way for the book's extended game with representation and interpretation. First Nicholas, and then his younger sister Caroline (introduced as a stereotypical goody-goody), attempts to interpret and influence their uncle Ludovic's behaviour on the basis of chance resemblances to events in Nicholas' book. This book within the book is never directly quoted, but in its notional existence it interacts with other generic, intertextual possibilities – vague assumptions about piracy, parrots, and hidden treasure, for example, and stories of moral reclamation with melodramatic happy endings when the villain resolves to reform. Ludovic himself embodies the melodramatic elements in his behaviour, but also in his speech, as he frequently employs a pretentious register and exclamatory syntax appropriate to some absurd melodrama, as, for example, 'What have I done? I've blotted my escutcheon. All my good resolutions gone, like snow upon the desert's dusty face.' (pp. 35–6).

The other major impetus for the narrative is a confusion over the relationship between signs and things which originates in Nicholas' overhearing of his parents' argument:

> 'Well, there's only one thing for it,' Andy Battle said firmly, 'they'll have to stay with old Ludovic.'
> Behind the chair Nick sat up taller in surprise. Ludovic was his father's brother. Nick had always wondered why his mother was suspicious of him.
> 'That pirate!' she exclaimed indignantly. 'I wouldn't trust him with a couple of hedgehogs, let alone two children.'
>
> (Mahy, *The Pirate Uncle*, pp. 10–11)

The parents are arguing about lifestyles, and there is a vast ideological gap between Gillian Battle's ideal of urban respectability and Ludovic Battle's unbuttoned life in his cottage by the sea. Her attitude is expressed clearly when the children ask how they will be able to recognize their uncle, and she replies, 'Look for a perambulating haystack with bare feet.' It further turns out that *pirate* is a signifier she habitually uses for Ludovic; he knows this, and plays on it to keep the children entertained during their stay. Soon after they meet he remarks, 'Has your mother ever called me a pirate? I'll bet she has, and she is right. I'm not just an uncle. I am a pirate too' (p. 20), and he gives the children the task of helping him reform. The book's narrative trajectory follows convergent paths, exploring the relationship between responsibility and freedom and their social encoding as physical appearance and public behaviour. To do this, the book's key signifier, *pirate*, becomes a focal point for numerous other signs, variously defining and misleading, which serve to blow out its conventional signified and show that the labelling functions of language must be treated with open-minded caution. If language functions to over-determine and over-categorize human lives, those lives become cramped and lacking in choice. The consequence of breaking down discrete categories is an expansion of human choice and possibility, a point the book clearly enunciates a few pages from the end while describing the wedding lunch for Ludovic and his neighbour Rosie:

> Nick knew . . . that, even when he and Caroline went home again, things would never be quite the same as they had been, for now they understood new things about each other and about themselves.
> Caroline, for example, had stepped into Uncle Ludovic's pirate story because there was a place for her in it, because she liked to play a part. She could be a pirate or a pirate-reformer. It all depended upon what life offered her. He, Nicholas, would never forget that beyond the streets and the warm glow of the street lights was the sand and the sea and Antofagasta, a city on the other side of the world with street lights of its own.
>
> (Mahy, *The Pirate Uncle*, p. 120)

The humanistic ideology underpinning *The Pirate Uncle* can be directly expressed in this way, but ultimately it is grounded in an awareness that it depends on the way social practice informs discoursal expressiveness. This idea about language is both the inspiration and the theme of Jan Mark's *Handles*.

The society inhabited by the main character of *Handles*, eleven-year-old Erica Timperley, is also firmly categorized:

> When Erica had been small, she had said that she wanted to be a nurse, because that was what everyone else wanted to be, then, and Mum had got it firmly fixed in her mind that this was still what she wanted to be. Nothing that Erica said or did could make her understand that all Erica wanted to be now was a motor-cycle mechanic. There was no point in mentioning it to Dad, either. He would not think it even possible for a woman to become a mechanic; it would be almost as unnatural as men having babies. Erica had not heard him say this, but she knew that it was what he thought. Craig [her brother], who was fifteen, really did want to become a nurse, but he too had not said anything to Dad. Erica hardly dared to guess what Dad might say about that, and neither did Craig.
>
> (Mark, *Handles*, p. 9)

Packed off to the country to spend the August holidays with her Aunt Joan Myhill and family, Erica enters a group whose life categories are even more restricted and restrictive. As she soon discovers, 'Every day was the same. After a week Erica understood that nothing was going to change, ever, at Hall Farm Cottage' (p. 32). As the story develops, it emerges that people's imprisonment in an unchanging temporality and their inability to see beyond the tiny boundaries of their lives is rooted not just in their parochialism but more particularly in a problem of language. The Myhills' lack of imagination is represented as a consequence of their inarticulateness, for the ability to name, to make jokes, and to play with the processes of signification is what seems to make people special. The book's title refers to the colloquial use of *handles* in the sense of a person's name, title, or nickname, and the book's narrative and thematic centre turns on the power inherent in name-giving and the relationship between *names* and *things* which is sometimes asserted, and sometimes altered, by the act of naming. Accepting the premise that the connection between names and things is arbitrary, throughout her book Mark explores the power of linguistic playfulness.

The main bestower of names is Lynden Wainwright (known as 'Elsie'), ex-teacher turned motor-cycle mechanic, though Erica herself has, incipiently, a similar command over language. Erica meets Elsie when she is sent on an errand to his workshop; from the outset he is associated with shifting signification:

> Erica picked up the message. It was in an old envelope, several times used. On the front it said, in typewritten letters, *To Mr C.J. Hemp*. Someone, presumably C.J. Hemp himself, had crossed out *C.J. Hemp* and written *P.D. Myhill*, which was Uncle Peter, underneath in blue biro. Uncle Peter had crossed out *P.D. Myhill* and scribbled, also underneath, in pencil, *Wainwright*. Erica took a pencil from the dresser and added an *s* to the original *Mr* so that the address now read *To Mrs Wainwright*, here and there.
>
> (Mark, *Handles*, p. 39)

Erica's addition in fact creates an error, since 'Elsie' is male, though there is a Mrs Wainwright, who makes a dramatic and crucial appearance towards the end of the book. More immediately, though, the reader watches the envelope resignify and degrade, as each name is more abbreviated and less formally inscribed (type to biro to pencil). The envelope is a concrete illustration of the process of reinscription that the book describes and which Elsie epitomizes.

Almost everything and everyone in Elsie's surroundings is subjected to his habit of renaming – everything, that is, except Erica
herself, who believes that one cannot belong until given a 'handle':
naming establishes identity, and, to Erica's thinking, acceptability.
The names Elsie bestows are based on physical resemblances, habits, functions, word-play and chance associations. It is principally
through Elsie's imagination and name-giving that the book's intertextuality functions: he is thoughtful, educated, well-read and,
above all, playful. For example, when the yard of the so-called in-
dustrial estate where he has his workshop is flooded he constructs
an intricate bridgework of planks and pallets to cross it. Erica's
view of the edifice is perceptive: 'It was undoubtedly a necessary arrangement, but Erica had the feeling that it was rather more
complex than it needed to be, and she suspected that Elsie had been
amusing himself while peforming a public service' (p. 124). He
names his structure the Golden Gate Bridge, and the chain of signification this creates is typical of Elsie's renamings: the similarity
between the planks and the real Golden Gate Bridge is, of course,
one of function, since they both cross water, but by transferring the
signifying phrase from one object to the other he also imaginatively
transforms the object signified.

Everyday events are also transformed by renaming them, especially by intertextual effects achieved by register shift and allusion.
When faced with the choice of driving some distance to pick up
someone whose bike has broken down or minding an undisciplined
child, Elsie chooses the former and turns it into a major event:

> Elsie came back into the cave [Erica's name for his workshop], square-
> jawed and stern.
>
> 'Right, you people,' he said, out of the corner of his mouth, 'the suc-
> cess of this operation depends on your pulling together. I'm relying on
> you to see this thing through.'
>
> 'What thing?' Bunny said crossly. 'Do talk straight for once, Else.'
> Erica knew better and leaped to attention with a salute that made her
> elbow crack.
>
> 'I'm depending on *you*,' Elsie said, 'and *him*, pointing to Bunny, 'to
> back me up, especially as I'm only doing it to keep that little monster
> out of my workshop. I myself am boldly going where no man has gone
> before. Wroxham, the final frontier . . .'
>
> 'Do give it a rest,' Bunny pleaded. 'You're out half the time, anyway.'
> 'No moral fibre,' Elsie said, sadly. 'I may be some time,' he continued
> through gritted teeth. 'Carry on, chaps.' He dived away across the

soupy ground and scrambled into the driving seat of the dreadful old
Ford Zephyr that Erica had taken for a wreck . . .

(Mark, Handles, p. 108–9)

Elsie's intertexts here are all British versions of heroic behaviour,
moving between the officer-class register which marks the military
jargon ('Right . . . pulling together . . . see this thing through .
. . Carry on, chaps') and the allusions to acts of individual heroism
culminating in the quotation of Captain Lawrence Oates' (fictitious)
last words, 'I may be some time.' The *inquit*-tags ('said, out of the
corner of his mouth' and so on) and Erica's quick response effectively cue the reader into the nature of Elsie's game, while Bunny's
refusal to play and the reference to 'that little monster' insist on the
continued presence of the mundane world. The recoding of Elsie's
actions here functions differently from the renamed bridge. It is another kind of iconoclasm, in that its banality mocks the intertexts,
and acts as a reminder that models of behaviour regarded as exemplary within Western culture are unrealistic in terms of the
experience of ordinary people. This is not altogether to deny the
value of individual achievement, but to relocate it within a less public sphere. A comparable example of combined register shift and
allusion in *The Pirate Uncle* might further clarify the effect in *Handles*. Uncle Ludovic, telling Nick that Rosie has agreed to marry him,
and wants the children present, explains,

> It seems Caroline thinks the whole thing is her idea. Apparently last
> night . . . Caroline whispered to Rosie that someone ought to marry
> me to save me from more piracy. She thought I might be redeemed by
> the love of a good woman.

(Mahy, The Pirate Uncle, p. 105)

The combination of pomposity and cliché in the concluding sentence opens a gap between expression and content, flattering
readers who have been long aware of Ludovic's play-acting and
who see that Caroline has naively confused play and earnest, and
literature and life. The incident is focused inwardly on the structure
and relationships of the narrative, and only minimally, if at all, offers a comment on the melodramatic cliché 'redeemed by the love of
a good woman'. Moreover, despite an immediate connection made
between Caroline's plan and Nicholas' book, the intertext a child is
more likely to access is some version of Madame Leprince de Beau-

mont's *Beauty and the Beast*, which Iona and Peter Opie have described as 'the prime example of the world-wide beast-marriage story' (1980, p. 179), and which is also, of course, the classic representation of disjunction between an outward sign and an inner essence. By comparison, Elsie's allusiveness is focused much more clearly at the possibility of absurdity inherent in its intertexts.

Although most other characters in the novel find Elsie's word-games annoying, they really are, in a sense, 'a public service' like his bridge, in that they do act as a constant reminder that the world can be looked at in more than one way. By the end of the novel, though, the reader has discovered that a primary inspiration for Elsie's playfulness is escapism, his own need to create a more attractive world than the one he knows, where his love of independence and motorcycles is paid for by his home life with a discontented and resentful wife and children who will never share in his imaginative play. It is for this reason, I think, that Erica does not get the 'handle' she so anxiously desires until the conversation in which she says goodbye to Elsie, and even then the naming falls flat:

'I never did get a handle,' Erica said.
'Well, you did,' said Elsie, 'but it was such a mouthful I never used it. Goodbye, Eroica Symphony.'
'What's that?'
'Music by Beethoven, haven't you heard of it?'
'No.'
'You've heard of *him*?'
'Yes.'
'That's all right then.' He hummed a few notes.
'And that's my handle?'
'It is here.'

(Mark, *Handles*, p. 156)

The renaming is a failure, for three reasons: it is generated by the mere phonemic similarity of Erica Timperley and Eroica Symphony rather than by some reorganization of signifier–signified relationship; it is an intertextual failure, since Erica has no useful associations to attach to it; and it is spatio-temporally restricted ('It is here'). The failure is thematically appropriate, though, since by the end of the book Erica doesn't need a handle, even if she doesn't realize this herself. Her own selfhood is sufficient, and so, finally, is her grasp on sign–thing relationships. In an early meditation on names (p. 66) she had thought that 'she was almost the only person she knew who did like her own name', and a conversation with

Bunny reveals her confidence with words and meanings (Bunny, who is arachniphobic, has just encountered a spider):

> Tactfully she took herself outside to where Bunny was gyrating strangely in the fireweed.
> 'That's a phobia,' he explained, sheepishly, as Erica tiptoed up behind him.
> 'I thought that was a spider,' Erica said.
> 'I'm not really frightened of them,' Bunny said. 'I just can't *stand* them.'
> Erica thought that this came to much the same thing.
>
> (Mark, *Handles*, pp. 80–1)

The conversation is symptomatic of Erica's understanding of how language works. Even in other exchanges where, because she is a child and/or an outsider, she is the weaker participant, she is still allowed a superior mental analysis of conversational pragmatics. In this exchange, she first makes a joke of Bunny's explanation by substituting a new signifier (*and* signified) for his 'phobia', and she then decodes his signifiers, 'frightened . . . can't stand', as pointing essentially to a single signified. These may be simple operations, but they represent considerable linguistic sophistication in an eleven-year-old, and communicate to readers (of about the same age) a sense of the positive power inhering in a good grasp of language.

Unlike the ending of *The Pirate Captain*, the ending of *Handles* is not overtly happy, and it encodes its values rather more subtly. Reader interpretation of the text is not subsumed here into character focalization so that the world is perceived as the characters have learned to see it, but rather readers go beyond Erica's feeling that she has had and lost something very special to grasp how special and valuable is Erica's own capacity to understand the world around her and to articulate that understanding.

INTERTEXTUALITY IN FANTASY AND FOLK TALE

Handles is about names. The power inherent in giving or knowing names has long been a prominent theme in the major children's literature genres of folk tale and fantasy, and these areas of discourse must inevitably function as intertexts for such works as *Handles* and *The Pirate Uncle*, even though they are themselves naturalistic in mode and make at most only stray connections with or allusions to other genres. In some of the most widely read fantasies the struggle of Good against Evil is won by knowing and uttering the true name of an antagonist (a motif I will discuss in more detail in Chapter 7). Clear examples of the motif occur in Ursula Le Guin's *A Wizard of Earthsea* (1968), when Ged must recognize and name the shadow which is his own *alter ego*, and in Lloyd Alexander's Celtic fantasy, *The Book of Three* (1964), in which the terrible Horned King actually dissolves when his true name is spoken. The relevance of such intertextual connections to *Handles* is perhaps most obviously seen in such an incident as the renaming of the main character at the beginning of *A Wizard of Earthsea*. This is the fantasy equivalent of Erica's desire, and in the fantasy context is explicitly encoded as the *rite de passage* which Erica implicitly seeks:

> As he entered the water clouds crossed the sun's face and great shadows slid and mingled over the water of the pool about him. He crossed to the far bank, shuddering with cold but walking slow and erect as he should through that icy, living water. As he came to the bank Ogion, waiting, reached out his hand and clasping the boy's arm whispered to him his true name: Ged.
>
> Thus was he given his name by one very wise in the use of power.
>
> (LeGuin, *A Wizard of Earthsea*, p. 12)

There is a theory of language implicit in this motif which posits an extraordinarily close bond between names and things, and an idea that a person somehow *is* his or her name, and, further, has no identity or even existence without it. Even when a name does not express such a single, unbroken relationship between surface and essence, the state of namelessness can express a radical exclusion from society. An unusual example of this kind of exclusion, a story in which name-giving constitutes the ultimate *rite de passage*, is the brief folk tale 'Short Hoggers', retold in Ruth Manning-Sanders' collection for children, *Scottish Folk Tales* (1976, pp. 93–5). 'Short Hoggers' is a folk ghost story, generically marked at the outset by the co-presence of the motifs of the restless spirit and the murderous stepmother, but also having as an obvious intertext the Christian doctrine of salvation (which it uses in a most theologically unsound way!). It is a story which expresses some mockery of bureaucracy and self-righteous morality, but its crux, both as story and theme, is naming. The only utterance made by the ghost in the indeterminate years of its haunting is the ditty,

Wae, wae is me, wi-oot a name,
I canna get going frae Whittinghame!

(Manning-Sanders, *Scottish Folk Tales*, p. 93)

The identification of namelessness and not-being is so strong here that, despite its infant innocence, the ghost is even barred entry to heaven:

> Saint Peter was holding a big book in one hand, and a quill pen in the other, and the first thing he said was, *'Name please?'*.
> 'I have nae name,' answered the little spirit.
> 'But,' says Saint Peter, 'no one can come in here without a name, because every soul has to be entered in my book. You must go back down to earth, my dear, and get you a name, before I can let you in.'

(Manning-Sanders, *Scottish Folk Tales*, p. 94)

There are two elements in the story which mark and threaten to perpetuate the ghost's state of unbeing: Saint Peter's bureaucratic application of the letter of the law, which should evoke an empathetic response to the ghost's plight in any reader who has been in a double-bind situation, and the unwillingness on the part of 'the good people of Whittinghame' to become involved, lest they endanger their own selfhood ('everyone believed that if you spoke to a ghost you would immediately die and become a ghost yourself'). The ghost's liberation is a chance event, brought about by the harmless anti-social behaviour of the town drunk, Sandy Macdougal:

> Sandy . . . looked the little ghost up and down, stared at its footless ragged stockings, laughed, touched his cap, and called out,
> 'Evening, evening! And how's all wi' ye, this braw evening, *Short Hoggers*?'

(Manning-Sanders, *Scottish Folk Tales*, p. 95)

This rather chance name-giving, which allows the little spirit to be entered in Saint Peter's book, contrasts with the deliberate act of naming in *A Wizard of Earthsea*, and up to a point suggests that signification is potent in itself, even when applied randomly. But there is more to it than this. If Sandy's actions are closely examined, it is evident that he looks carefully at the person, notes a particular attribute, responds, acknowledges, and addresses. In his fashion, in other words, he goes through the first steps of recognizing the selfhood of the other. The text acknowledges Sandy's own right to be

himself, in that no adverse judgement is expressed about his drun-
kenness, and he does free both the ghost and the town from their
mutual and symbiotic torments.

MEDIEVALISM AS INTERTEXTUALITY

A type of intertextuality I have not yet considered may be exemplified by the related discourses of Arthuriana and medievalism,
which I referred to earlier. There is a distinction between the profes-
sional medievalist's idea of the Middle Ages and its literature and
the vague ideas about things medieval which, in various forms,
have pervaded Western culture throughout post-medieval times,
and which I have termed *medievalism*. This is a complex subject, but
in essence medievalism involves the invention of an alterity of time
and place which, although more primitive, is also somehow nobler,
and of a society whose beliefs, structures, rules and obligations are
clearer and more open than those of the society inhabited by the
writers and their audiences. The function of this non-existent place
is to comment on the decadence of the present and its values.

As a broad discourse, medievalism is perhaps to be approached
warily. Its penchant for allegory and fable, often packaged in consolatory and sentimental language, has at times made it a powerful
exponent of class-based ideologies, masquerading under such humanistic tenets as 'the underlying, unchanging nature of mankind'.
One of the more notable modern examples, Tolkien's *The Lord of the
Rings* (1966), enjoyed an astounding cult-following through the
1960s and 1970s, though there were always some voices to question
its ideological bases and to claim, as, for example, Michael Moor-
cock has done recently, that it 'is a pernicious confirmation of the
values of a morally bankrupt middle class' (1987, p. 125).

I would suggest that a work employing the discourse of medievalism must consciously interrogate its own intertextuality in
order to avoid the fallacy of 'unchanging human nature' and to confront the social construction of significance. This programme is
achieved in a remarkable way in Peter Dickinson's *Merlin Dreams*
(1988), a handsomely produced book, beautifully illustrated by
Alan Lee. The book is a collection of stories, presented as the
'dreams' of Merlin where he lies buried for eternity beneath a rock.

The reader enters *Merlin Dreams* through a complex frame. First, an epigraph sets out the pre-text for the frame story, an episode from Malory's *Morte d'Arthur* which tells how Merlin was betrayed and imprisoned by a lover. Next, the story is retold by Dickinson, but in such a way as to problematize setting and character motivation: the bare, deserted moorland where the incident occurs defies spatio-temporal location, and Merlin's immurement is as much his own doing as his companion's. As Merlin begins to dream at the end of this section the first dream – about a killer-priest guarding a holy pool – slides unfinished into a second – about a medieval knight guarding a ford. In this way Dickinson signals that his book is largely an exploration of the situations within which archetypes are articulated into discourse and change their meanings. Finally, the first story within the frame, 'Knight Errant', tells of a knight who must overcome two guardians of wells and the guardian of a ford, but this knight is 'a false knight and a traitor and a coward' (p. 31), and one of the important functions of the story is to deconstruct the convention of the 'pure and noble knight' (p. 31). At this particular point, Dickinson uses a register derived from Malory (evident both in the signifiers and in the excessive use of the co-ordinator 'and'), perhaps as a reminder that Malory had already done this work of deconstruction but it had been ignored. So while *Merlin Dreams* may create, as the dust jacket claims, 'a remarkable world of mediaeval fantasy', its first moves are to strip away the easy associations and assumptions of medievalism and to signal that a different kind of intertextuality is in operation.

The constant concern of the frame, which reappears between any two of the stories, is with the interrelationships of history, legend, art, imagination and the world. This becomes increasingly evident as the intertexts move away from Malory to Celtic lore and 'history' (incorporating, for example, Rosemary Sutcliff) to embrace all time and space. The frame also, importantly, locates the stories within a sense of the power of language to change the world, or at least to change how the world is interpreted. The stories themselves are principally about power and its temptations and abuses, and about the perpetuation of Selfhood. All these things come together in the final story, 'Enchantress', which tells, in William Blake's phrase, of the 'mind-forg'd manacles' of a tyranny, perpetuated by belief in it and defeated by a refusal to make that act of belief. Through their interrogation of tradition, the first and final stories act as another, inner frame.

This final story begins in a high Gothic mode: the Enchantress lives in a mist-shrouded castle surrounded by a dense wood, and uses rooks and bats to spy on the surrounding people, her subjects. Any beautiful child born in the district is hers: she rewards the parents with rich crops, and in the child's fourteenth year takes it for herself. In some unspecified way, her perpetuation is effected by absorbing the child. The Enchantress suggests many meanings: she is Hope and Fear; she is Tradition and Superstition; she is God.

When she tries to take the beautiful young girl Fara, Fara's best friend, the 'utterly hideous' Dan, manages to accompany her. Dan is gifted with, and symbolizes, the power of insight: when he looks at people with his blue eye, he sees 'right through to the centre of their being', and when he looks with his brown, he sees 'what they might have been . . . or what they ought to be, or what they could never be'. To enter the castle, Dan has to get past three lots of guards, which are obviously drawn from classical mythology rather than from medieval tradition: a centaur, three mermaids, and a three-headed dog (that is, a version of Cerberus). He defeats each of these by attacking the very ground of their subjectivity: by pointing out that their being is impossible, and therefore resides not in any pre-existent selfhood but in pure intersubjectivity, he threatens them with not-being, and only revives them at the last minute with the quasi-Cartesian formula, 'You [exist] because I suppose you to.' Dan's power also lies in the power of names, as Dickinson also draws on the traditions about names discussed above. Even here, though, he twists it: unlike the spirit in 'Short Hoggers', Dan first gets past the old man who keeps the book of names because his name has been blotted out and doesn't appear there, and then defeats the Enchantress with that knowledge. The text is self-evident, so at this point I will simply quote from it:

> 'I know your name,' said Dan. 'I know your name, and you do not. You do not know your own name.' . . .
>
> 'There is one syllable of your name you do not know,' said Dan. 'It is covered with a blot in the book. It is my name. Because your name is all the names in the book. All our names. You are us. You are our dream. You are our nightmare.' . . .
>
> 'You exist because we suppose you to exist,' said Dan. 'Now I suppose you not to.'
>
> There was a moment like the stopping of a heart, then all light vanished. A wail, dwindling to a far sigh. Blackness.
>
> (Dickinson, *Merlin Dreams*, p. 161)

The last lines cited are, I think, an echo of the climactic moment in the third volume of *The Lord of the Rings*:

> And into the heart of the storm, with a cry that pierced all other sounds, tearing the clouds asunder, the Nazgûl came, shooting like flaming bolts, as caught in the fiery ruin of hill and sky they crackled, withered, and went out.
>
> (Tolkien, *The Lord of the Rings*, pp. 236–7)

Dickinson has simultaneously evoked Tolkien and, as it were, supposed him not to exist. More importantly, though, the ending of 'Enchantress' opposes the consolatory ending of *The Lord of the Rings*, for Dan's victory is, of course, not the end, since the Enchantress regains her being as soon as people again suppose her to exist; freedom from tyranny is a contingent state, and one that must be constantly defended. Tyranny is not just a political phenomenon, but also social and cultural, and the final story of *Merlin Dreams* leaves its readers with an assertion of the power of the intellect over tradition, over intertextuality, and, indeed, over being itself. Like the other stories in the book, 'Enchantress' is not difficult, but it does point the way for us backwards into a book which is one of the most interesting statements about textuality, intertextuality and culture available to young readers.

CONCLUSION

The observation that meaning is not the product of a self-contained linguistic system, but emerges as part of a complex interconnection of language, society, and a variety of discourses has particular significance for children's literature, which exists at the intersection of a number of other discourses, particularly those of: traditional narrative forms and genres; specialized contents (such as mythology, and so on); and ideological discourses. The third of these groups in mediating between the first two and readers seeks to determine how texts will be interpreted and what socializing and acculturating effects they might have. Thus intertextuality is exploited to inculcate knowledge about contemporary culture and to illustrate how that knowledge is to be used.

Because meaning is produced from the interrelationships between audience, text, other texts, and the socio-cultural determinations of significance, all texts can be said to inhabit an intertextual space. Moreover, the mutual interactions of texts are comparable with the intersubjectivity which shapes individual subjectivity in day-to-day existence. This becomes more apparent when one discourse space overtly embraces both a pre-text and focused text in such a way that the significance of the narrative is situated not in the focused text but in the process of interaction between the texts. Intertextuality thus has the effect of drawing readers' attention to the reading process itself, and thence to such issues of representation, narration, and art–life relationships as the impact of language and convention on subjectivity, and the impact that society and its changing circumstances have on significance.

Intertextual function is not restricted to the relationships between *texts* defined in a narrow sense, but also operates in the large sense of a cultural discourse, especially with reference to the relationships between language, signs and culture. The product can be a complex within which texts, and texts and society, interact, characters within those texts are represented as working out their own subjectivities through intersubjective relations, and readers are enabled to experiment with subject positions different from those of their everyday lives, in a context which insists on the fictiveness of its representations.

Intertextuality, by making relationships between different cultures and different periods, can act as a critique of current social values. This is achieved in contrasting ways in *Handles* and *Merlin Dreams*. The former suggests, for example, that models of behaviour regarded as exemplary within Western culture are unrealistic in terms of the experience of ordinary people. The latter in part also makes a similar comment by presenting deconstructed versions of heroic themes within idealistic 'medieval' settings, but also probes more deeply into the question of how history, legend, art, and 'culture' in general, are implicated in the social construction of significance. The theme is clearly presented in the final story in its study of the relationship between individuality, intersubjectivity and subjection.

Finally, intertextuality frequently takes the specific form of parody or travesty of a pre-text, and its purpose often seems to be an iconoclastic gesture attempting to subvert what is perceived as a dominant discourse. This aspect overlaps with the topic of my next chapter, which examines a special kind of intertextual mode, carnivalesque interrogative. This mode is intertextual since it proceeds

by parodying and mocking recognizable social forms and structures
and literary genres and texts.

TAKING IT FURTHER

It must be stressed that the study of intertextuality is not to be confused with mere source-study. Rather, it is concerned with how
meaning is produced at points of interaction. One of its principal
implications for reading is that by invoking multiple perspectives a
narrative discourse encourages critical reading, building in 'distancing' strategies which enable the reading self to operate in dialogue
both with points of view articulated within the discourse and with
social practices. Excellent examples produced for very young audiences are John Burningham's 'Shirley' books, *Come away from the
water, Shirley* (1977) and *Time to get out of the bath, Shirley* (1978),
where the fantasy life the young protagonist opposes to her parents'
unimaginative and restrictive existence depends heavily on intertextuality. The possibilities for further studies of intertextuality are
almost limitless; I will suggest only a few additional directions here.

A very accessible area is contemporary fairy-tale discourse, since,
as Zipes has shown (1983 and elsewhere), fairy tales invariably represent the 'same' story imbued with the ideologies of the producing
society. Collections of 'fractured' fairy tales, with their iconoclastic
mocking of traditional stories, may be examined productively to ex-
pose both a rejected ideology and the social presuppositions which
enable the iconoclasm. Comparable effects are seen in Zipes's very
useful collection, *Don't Bet on the Prince* (1986), where the masculinist suppositions of conventional fairy tale are subjected to interrogation by being retold in a mildly feminist discourse. Another
productive study might be to examine the political implications pervading Terry Jones's *Fairy Tales* (1981), a collection of original
stories using traditional patterns. There are no identifiable sources
in either the Zipes or the Jones, but both collections are intertextually very rich and very thought-provoking.

Other kinds of traditional materials commonly used to inculcate
values are biblical story and heroic legend. In these the distinction
between source and re-telling may not function intertextually.
Readers might like to compare Catherine Storr's excellent series of
Bible stories, whose purpose seems to be well-told recounts, first

with her own fractured fairy tales in *It Shouldn't Happen to a Frog* (1984), and then with Peter Dickinson's remarkable retelling of Old Testament stories in *City of Gold* (1980), where biblical texts become productively intertextual. Note especially how Dickinson uses a variety of narrative frames to achieve this. More elusively intertextual is Ted Hughes's *Tales of the Early World* (1988) which initiates, for example, a good-humoured intertextual dialogue between creationism and evolutionary theory.

Heroic legend may be recounted in order to affirm some desired (usually masculinist) values, but modern narratives more characteristically seek to disclose the radical disorderliness of heroic codes. This may be explored in the various versions for children of the Old English *Beowulf* (see Mills, 1986), and especially if these are put together with Louise Lawrence's *The Warriors of Taan* (1986) and Robyn Klein's *Birk the Berserker* (1987), both of which use cultural contact to interrogate a heroic ethos.

Finally, many books have intertextual relationships with less specific textual contexts. A book about families will interrelate with other books identifiable as 'family stories', and such linkings may be completely aleatory. Any story about running away from home will suggest links ranging from 'The Gingerbread Man' to *Huckleberry Finn*. And a book such as Tim Winton's *Lockie Leonard, Human Torpedo* (1989) has clear intertextual links with the specialized discourse of surfing and the recognizable 'text' which is an Australian beach (see Fiske 1983).

In all such explorations, it is important to remember that the ideological assumptions of the producing culture will always be inscribed within the discoursal processes whereby the 'source', whether it is a known story or a narrative pattern, is re-presented. Intertextuality will project the meaning of a text as a dialogue amongst these elements.

FURTHER READING

Intertextuality is a concept only recently formulated, and it has probably not yet settled into a generally accepted meaning. Discussions I have found most helpful are Birch (1989), Culler (1981), Miller (1985), and Riffaterre (1980a; 1981). The concept has not been applied to children's fiction, with the exception of Hunt (1988b) and

Stephens (1990a – in part an earlier version of the opening pages of this chapter). For political ideologies in children's literature, see Sutherland (1985).

FOUR

Ideology, carnival and interrogative texts

In the previous chapter I suggested that one potential function of intertextuality is to construct for the reader both specific subject positions and positions of subjection. In this chapter I wish to ask whether there are other kinds of textual practices which might offer freer roles to the reader.

As always, what is at issue is the relationship between text and world. The educational and domestic structures of Western societies on the whole aspire to encourage their children to grow up as reasonable, creative, autonomous and achieving human beings, and these ideals are furthered by the ideological positions implicit in the literature produced for children. The ideals, however, may often conflict with notions of social co-operation, which require children to obey rules (which may seem unreasonable) and to accept subordinate roles in decision-making processes and in conversational exchanges. It is also widely acknowledged that social practices and social rules still vary on gender bases, in such areas as types and motives of discipline and tolerance of behaviour in some sense 'deviant' (Broverman *et al* 1970; Walkerdine 1985). Such variations may also include self-contradiction, as when boys are encouraged to engage in mischievous behaviour for which they are subsequently punished (the semantic ambivalence of terms associated with such behaviour – *villain*, *rogue* and Australian *larrikin* – is in itself informative), and as when girls are encouraged to develop docile 'feminine' roles which in masculinist society are at the same time given pejorative denotations.

Since about 1960 there has appeared a variety of books for children which broadly share an impulse to create roles for child characters which interrogate the normal subject positions created for children within socially dominant ideological frames. I am going to refer to these as 'carnivalesque' texts, since they function to interrogate official culture in ways comparable to the traits of carnival identified in the work of Mikhail Bakhtin (1965). These texts may be divided into three types. First, those which offer the characters 'time out' from the habitual constraints of society but incorporate a safe return to social normality. Widely read examples are *Harry the Dirty Dog* (1956) by Gene Zion and Margaret Bloy Graham, and Maurice Sendak's *Where the Wild Things Are* (1963). This type shares many traits with adventure stories in which adults are not present to intervene in events, and I will shortly discuss Edith Nesbit's *Five Children and It* (1902) as a precursor with carnivalesque tendencies but moral outcomes. The type may also be appropriated for didactic purposes, as in Robert Byrd's *Marcella Was Bored* (1985), but is usually posited on some flouting of an adult prohibition. The second type strives through gentle mockery to dismantle socially received ideas and replace them with their opposite, privileging weakness over strength, for example. Babette Cole's *Prince Cinders* (1987) and Anthony Browne's *Willy the Wimp* (1984) illustrate this type. The third type, which is likely to be more recent and of British origin, consists of books which are endemically subversive of such things as social authority, received paradigms of behaviour and morality, and major literary genres associated with children's literature. Examples are *Out of the Oven* (1986) by Jan Mark (text) and Antony Maitland (illustrations) and Jan Needle's *Wagstaffe the Wind-up Boy* (1987).

While the books I have mentioned vary greatly amongst themselves, they share qualities which characterize carnivalesque and interrogative texts. Before discussing any of these books in detail, I will attempt to describe what forms those qualities take in children's literature.

CARNIVALESQUE AND INTERROGATIVE TEXTS

Carnival

Carnival in children's literature is grounded in a playfulness which situates itself in positions of nonconformity. It expresses opposition to authoritarianism and seriousness, and is often manifested as parody of prevailing literary forms and genres, or as literature in non-canonical forms. Its discourse is often idiomatic, and rich in a play of signifiers which foregrounds the relativity of sign–thing relationships, and hence the relativity of prevailing 'truths' and ideologies. Children's literature does not make extensive use of the abusive language or the insulting words or expressions generally characteristic of the carnivalesque in its breaking of the norms of official speech, but it does have linguistic and narrative resources through which to mock and challenge authoritative figures and structures of the adult world – parents, teachers, political and religious institutions – and some of the (often traditionally male) values of society such as independence, individuality, and the activities of striving, aggression and conquest. In more specific terms, official, adult authority regulates such things as: modes of behaviour expected at home and at school – obedience, approved table manners, language uses and varieties (taboos, etc.); subject–object positions in adult–child conversations (with special applications of Gricean maxims); orderliness, sleeping hours, tidiness and cleanliness. Hence playful and, to some extent, taboo language is used to disclose ways in which adult incompetence masks itself as adult authority, and more generally to construct subject positions in opposition to society's official structures of authority (what Althusser has termed Ideological State Apparatuses).

The 'hero' of an interrogative text is sometimes a clown or a fool, and as such may function to render problematic common social assumptions and presuppositions by blurring the borders between the serious and comic, and between the 'reality' that is and the ideality which is constructed. Such figures also contribute to the self-conscious textuality of interrogative texts, since by drawing attention to roles and role-playing they draw attention to the text itself as a construct. Both *Prince Cinders* and *Willy the Wimp* exploit easily recognized genres to transpose social ideals into comic inversions and heroes into their parodic doublets.

Finally, the interrogative texts of children's literature allow a significant space for what Bakhtin termed 'the material bodily principle' – the human body and its concerns with food and drink (commonly in hyperbolic forms of gluttony and deprivation), sexuality (usually displaced into questions of undress) and excretory functions (usually displaced into opportunities for getting dirty). Meals and feasts, for example, are an important part of human culture, and have a unique and significant role in children's literature (Katz 1980). Official meals, that is, meals conducted at times and places determined by adult authority, reinforce the existing patterns of things and social hierarchies, and assert certain values as stable, normal and moral. An early reference in *Five Children and It* to the children being 'caught and cleaned for tea' (p. 13) discloses, despite its jokiness, the prevailing attitude that meals are part of the process whereby children are civilized and socialized in order to take their place in adult society. Katz (p. 193) has observed that the practice of using meals as a measure of the child's adjustment to the social order is especially pronounced in English children's literature. The carnivalesque children's feast – whether 'midnight feast' or birthday party or food-fight – celebrates a temporary liberation from official control over the time, place and manner in which food is consumed. In *Five Children and It*, where food is of central concern to the main characters without being carnivalized, the baby is allowed to be revolting at mealtimes but a somewhat arch distance is maintained when the older children, compelled to eat invisible food, regress to primitive methods:

> The next moment all the others were . . . opening and shutting their mouths an inch or so from the bare- looking table. Robert captured a slice of mutton, and – but I think I will draw a veil over the rest of this painful scene. It is enough to say that they all had enough mutton, and that when Martha [the maid] came to change the plates she said she had never seen such a mess in all her born days.
>
> (Nesbit, *Five Children and It*, p. 127)

I will return to the function of food in this book shortly, and will later pursue the relationship between carnival and the grotesque in another context.

The interrogative text

The qualities of the interrogative text centre on the construction of reader subject positions. Positions which readers might possibly assume may be constructed principally by language (the play of signifiers which constitutes a joke, for example, or the selection of a particular register), or principally by an action or events, or by a combination, as I will demonstrate shortly. Action-focused outrageousness in more recent texts may move more deeply into taboo areas in response to the steady shift in the boundaries of taboo during this century.

Other characteristics of interrogative texts include a tendency to employ a range of discourses which may function oppositionally or dialectically, effecting a multiplicity of unresolved points of view on both micro-discoursal and macro-discoursal levels. Such an element of indeterminacy may operate in conjunction with a tendency to employ textual strategies which undermine the illusion of fiction-ality by drawing attention to the nature of the text as text. This latter strategy is also in its own right a characteristic of interrogative texts, and may range across varieties of narrator intrusiveness, self-con-scious intertextuality, and broadly metafictional strategies. Finally, as Belsey (1980) points out, interrogative texts may be apt to employ narrative structures which do not lead to that form of closure which in classic realism is also a final disclosure of theme, moral, or tran-scendent significance.

The subject positions made available to readers also tend to dis-courage simple identification with the subject position of one or more of the characters within the text. That is to say, readers' atti-tudes to the main character, for example, and to the ways in which that character relates with the world of the text and its events, may shift amongst such positions as empathy, delight, superiority, criti-cism, outrage, revulsion, and so on, and may even combine two or more in one response. Shock, delight and revulsion, for example, are all likely responses to the following extract's breaches of taboos relating to language, behaviour and respect for adults, and its blur-ring of the human and the animal (or even bestial):

Wagstaffe's mum was even more dreadful than his dad . . ..
    'You should have been drowned at birth,' she told him once. 'What a pity you're not a puppy.'
    Wagstaffe thought it was a pity too. If she'd tried to drown him he could have bitten her. Or at least peed on her leg. He peed on her leg anyway.

(Needle, *Wagstaffe the Wind-up Boy*, p. 27)

The irreverent attitude towards a parent may evoke a mixture of shock and pleasure, though the element of shock is likely to be quickly mitigated by the cruel streak revealed in the mother's thought processes. The two parts of her utterance are a good example of the impact of inferencing on a reader's construction of the text, since there is no actual or logical connection between the two parts other than the associative linking of 'drowned at birth' and 'puppy'. The effect is to disclose the mother's mind as one which readily and unreflectively makes such connections. Readers are thus well placed attitudinally for the cohesive continuation into Wagstaffe's thoughts ('a pity . . . drown') with its logical climax in 'could have bitten her'. The chain does not end there, however, but posits an alternative and more comic possibility in the form of a taboo event expressed through a taboo signifier, *peed on her leg*. The reader's choice from amongst a variety of points of view from which to regard the discourse reaches its widest range with the final movement in the sequence where Wagstaffe's conditionally imagining himself as a puppy is transformed into self-consciously acting like a puppy: 'He peed on her leg anyway.' The effect of immediately repeating an utterance almost in its entirety, but with a drastic shift of its meaning, is very comic. The act itself, however, is outrageous, and further complicates reader attitude towards Wagstaffe. He may invite some measure of sympathy, but not empathy; there is some splitting of attitude between the character and the action, and between the acting subject and the object acted upon, but there is no one position which can be said to contain all the others. The effect is to discourage identification with the character as subject and to situate the reader as subject firmly outside the text.

Before moving on to discuss a number of texts in some detail, I give in table form a survey of the main characteristics of interrogative texts, set out to show the ways in which they *tend* to be distributed across the three types of interrogative text with which I am concerned (Figure 4.1, p. 126). While I think the distribution suggested will generally apply, it must be stressed that I am not offering it as a definitive or defining schema.

DIDACTIC LIMITATIONS ON CARNIVAL: EDITH NESBIT'S *FIVE CHILDREN AND IT*

Carnivalesque children's literature is, of course, invariably written and produced by adults, and can well mask a didactic and educational purpose. Thus a text which appears to employ many of the characteristics of an interrogative text may turn out to be ideologically conservative. I shall begin this discussion by considering such a text, Edith Nesbit's *Five Children and It*, which seems to use an interrogative, carnivalesque mode, but does so in such a way as to produce disempowered reader positions subjected to the text's di-

	Time Out	Value Inversion	Transgression
Mood	Playful	Playful	Playful
Structure	Return	Overcoming	Separation
Ending	+Closure +Disclosure	+Closure +Disclosure	+−Closure +−Disclosure
Mode	Serious	Parodic	Parodic/satiric
Register	Idiomatic, acceptable	Ironic, citational	Idiomatic, taboo
Textuality	−Self-reflexive	+Self-reflexive	+Self-reflexive
Focus	Social familial	Social personal	social political familial
Effect	Interrogate → understanding	Interrogate → revision	Interrogate → rejection
Characters	Subject → Subjection	Subjection → Subject	Subjection → Subject
Roles	Hero	Non-hero	Anti-hero

Figure 4.1: Characteristics of interrogative texts

dactic ideology. Since its reissue as a Puffin in 1959, this book has been reprinted over twenty times, though Lukens (1986, p. 178) suggests that it is probably not much read by contemporary children, perhaps because of its sentimental and condescending tone. The Rustins (1987), who have written sympathetically about *Five Children and It*, balance Nesbit's unusual ability 'to enter a child's world in its own terms' with the comment that 'she was born in 1858, and also shared the customary moral seriousness of her time' (1987, p. 66). Thus while the book has many traits which seem to link it to the carnivalesque text, such as a self-consciousness about its own textuality, its overall thrust, and especially its moral didacticism and lack of even implicit questioning of received (adult) social values, must exclude it from that category. The opening chapter, though, is replete with elements which seem to invite a reading as carnivalesque. Mother and children view the holiday house antithetically, she regarding it as 'rather inconvenient', while to them it is 'a sort of Fairy Palace set down in an Earthly Paradise' (with obvious reference to the fantasies of William Morris).

The countryside is represented as an escape both from the naughtiness in children consequent upon urban living and from the battery of adults which exists to reprove that naughtiness ('fathers and mothers, aunts, uncles, cousins, tutors, governesses, and nurses'); indeed there 'were no rules [stated or implicit] about not going to places and not doing things'. Finally, both parents are called away for separate reasons (notably linked to gender roles: Father on business; Mother to care for an ill 'Granny'), thus completely freeing the children from direct parental constraint (the children have a very superior attitude to the adult servants left to take care of them and whose disciplinary powers are generally ineffective). It is when all of these factors are in place that the children enter a gravel-pit and meet the Psammead, a Sand-fairy with the power to grant wishes. Until liberated from adult surveillance they had not dared enter the pit, 'for fear father should say they mustn't play there'. The Psammead thus has the potential to represent the operation of childhood imagination, and its behaviour is sometimes quite child-like, but ultimately it functions as a kind of super-ego which asserts the values and order of the adult world and discloses that childhood imagination is acutely limited.

The functions of the Psammead are largely self-evident, but their effect is defined more tellingly in the context of the metalinguistic and metafictional aspects of *Five Children and It*. The story is told by a narrator who emphasizes the text's fictionality by drawing attention to her own role as creator and commentator, by connecting the behaviour of her characters with role-models derived from books which are in turn characterized as conventional constructs, and by little outbreaks of humour based on a sense of the arbitrary links between signs and things. The self-consciousness of the narrator's role is pervasive, but is clearly exemplified early in Chapter 1 when she enacts, in tongue-in-cheek fashion, a deliberate decision to write fantasy rather than realism. Having implied a narratee who has much in common with the book's fictional characters, she imagines that the consequences of a story about 'all the ordinary things that the children did – just the kind of things you do yourself, you know', including 'being tiresome', would be that 'your aunts would perhaps write in the margin of the story with a pencil, "How true!" or "How like life!" and you would see it and very likely be annoyed'. Realist texts, according to this account, are both directly representational and didactic. The alternative is to produce a text which denies the 'facts' propagated by adult authority:

> Grown-up people find it very difficult to believe really wonderful things, unless they have what they call proof. But children will believe almost anything, and grown-ups know this. That is why they tell you that the earth is round like an orange, when you can see perfectly well that it is flat and lumpy; and why they say that the earth goes round the sun, when you can see for yourself any day that the sun gets up in the morning and goes to bed at night like a good sun as it is, and the earth knows its place, and lies as still as a mouse. Yet I daresay you believe all that about the earth and the sun, and so you will find it quite easy to believe that before Anthea and Cyril and the others had been a week in the country they had found a fairy.
>
> (Nesbit, *Five Children and It*, p. 14)

It is not easy in this to disentangle the joke shared with the narratee and the condescending joke at the narratee's expense. The invitation is to discard adult knowledge and replace it with a carnivalesque inversion, replacing the authoritatively known with the empirically perceived (what 'you can see perfectly well'). But those empirical perceptions are in turn encoded as childish perceptions. First, 'like an orange' already re-encodes the unimaginably large as something familiar and easily grasped, and then 'flat and lumpy' as a descriptor of the earth is 'child-like' in its inadequacy. Secondly, the anthropomorphic (mis-)description of the movements of the sun and earth appropriates the language of adults talking down to children while putting them to bed, and through this reinstates the normal social hierarchy even at the centre of carnival, implying that the narratee 'like a good . . .' and 'still as a mouse' also 'knows its place'. The passage thus simultaneously shares a joke with and patronizes the narratee. I think the same effect is present in the carnivalesque illogic of the conclusion: if you choose to believe one thing contrary to empirical perception on the basis of adult authority, then you can just as easily believe another; for everything, and therefore nothing, is knowable on these terms. The result is that adult authority becomes reinscribed in the text as the source of knowledge. It is then not surprising to find that the narrator–narratee dialogue sustained throughout the book normally has a didactic function, appearing most obviously in such addresses as 'You know grown-up people often say they do not like to punish you, and that they only do it for your own good, and that it hurts them as much as it hurts you . . .'. I've broken the sentence there to ask what an interrogative text might do with it: the three co-ordinate clauses attached to 'say' seem to form a meaningful sequence in the presentation of discipline in the parent–child relationship, and from a modern perspective the sequence might even seem overdefensive and hence self-dismantling. An interrogative text might therefore use the sequencing to focus on the basis of discipline in that relationship, and to reach a final clause which links oppositionally to what has gone before, whereas Nesbit concludes the sentence by affirming all of its components, 'and this is really very often the truth' (p 111). It is a long way from here to the almost anarchic carnivalesque of Jan Needle's *Wagstaffe the Wind-up Boy*, where sequencing of such a kind is apt to meet with disjunction:

> [Wagstaffe's father] was a sensible, boring person who wore a suit and never let you play with him. He said that eating carrots made you see in the dark, and watching TV made you blind.
>
> He was a liar.
>
> (Needle, *Wagstaffe the Wind-up Boy*, p. 26)

The other elements of textual self-consciousness can be demonstrated more briefly. The connections between the characters and other books are treated most overtly in Chapters 6 and 7, the episode in which the children are granted the wish to be in a besieged castle. Both the castle and the arms of the besieging soldiers, as extensions of the children's world-knowledge, are a bookish mish-mash, Nesbit's ironic comment on the eclectic habits of modern medievalism whereby elements are randomly drawn from vast tracts of time and space. Robert, we are told,

> was dumb with admiration, and it all seemed to him perfectly correct, because he knew no more of heraldry or archaeology than the gifted artists who usually drew the pictures for the historical romances. The scene was indeed 'exactly like a picture'.
>
> (Nesbit, *Five Children and It*, p. 116)

The wide-ranging irony here implies a shared sense of a proper hierarchy of genres (which carnival seeks rather to dismantle) and an assumption that facts are knowable and that children do not know them (so that the narratee simultaneously shares the joke and is disempowered). Once again, this seems to me symptomatic of a presupposition about childhood which pervades the book. The same kind of ambivalence, whereby the narratee is invited to share a joke which in the end is at the narratee's expense, informs the allusions to books as models of behaviour which occur throughout *Five Children and It*. A couple of other examples are: '[Anthea] opened the dining room window and climbed out. It would have been easier to go out by the door, but the window was more romantic, and less likely to be noticed by Martha'; and 'So [Cyril] stood up, and squared his shoulders and tried to look noble, like the boys in books that no one can look in the face of and doubt that they come of brave and noble families and will be faithful to the death'. What seems to me to be emerging from this analysis is that, delightful as the story may be, *Five Children and It* cannot offer its readers a subject position outside the text based on a different or better knowledge, because it constructs childhood as a period of helplessness, ignorance, and incompetence.

The final type of textual self-consciousness to be considered is the touches of humour based on the arbitrary links between signs and things. There are many examples, especially within the Psammead's discourse, though a couple will suffice here. At the first meeting with the Psammead, the process of identification is as follows:

> 'Do you mean to tell me seriously you don't know a Psammead when you see one?'
> 'A Sammyadd? That's Greek to me.'

'So it is to everyone,' said the creature sharply. 'Well, in plain English, then, a *Sand-fairy*. Don't you know a Sand-fairy when you see one?'

(Nesbit, *Five Children and It*, p. 19)

This is the first lesson the children receive in the knowledge that to
be able to *name* something is not to determine its nature or meaning.
The message inheres in the double representation of unstable signifier–signified relationships, first a signifier with apparently
unrelated signifieds ('Greek'), and then two signifiers for a single
(but nevertheless still undetermined) signified ('Psammead' and
'Sand-fairy'). This linguistic playfulness is another common feature
of the interrogative text, but here it is directed not towards a problematizing of the world's knowability and stability but towards
disclosing the cognitive limitations of the would-be knowers. An
even stronger example, now with an explicitly moral import, occurs
when the children are making their second wish:

'What's the next wish?'
'We want,' said Robert slowly, 'to be rich beyond the dreams of something or other.'
'Avarice,' said Jane.
'So it is,' said the Fairy unexpectedly. 'But it won't do you much
good, that's one comfort,' it muttered to itself. 'Come – I can't go beyond
dreams, you know!'

(Nesbit, *Five Children and It*, p. 37)

The play of signifiers here has been very firmly subordinated to the
making of a moral point, even while the wider discourse seems oblivious to the social ideology underpinning that morality. The
children are mocked in three stages here: in Robert's mouthing of a
cliché while ignorant of its whole formulation; in Jane's completion
of the formula, but with a signifier which to her is empty of significance; and in the Fairy's confirmation of Jane's term, though in its
full sense, and in the accompanying remark about the pointlessness
of their wish. But if my reading of it is correct, the dialogue also discloses the implicit assumptions made in a capitalist society about
the regulation of desire for material goods. Avarice is a vice when
society's have-nots wish to be rich beyond the dreams of . . .
something or other.

This brings me back to the function of the Psammead in the
story. As I remarked above, the Psammead has an ambivalent function, in that it both grants the children their wishes, no matter how

irresponsible or thoughtless they are, and regulates the effect of those wishes, so that the children are always brought to see the moral lesson inherent in the frustrating attempts to indulge their desires. The importance of food in children's literature is clearly seen here, in that the getting, eating, or being deprived of food is a central focus in most of the episodes. In the first, for example, the vain desire to be 'beautiful as the day' renders them unrecognizable to the servants and hence leaves them hungry and thirsty. The Psammead at times recommends that they merely wish for food, and this helps focus how the whole series of adventures documents the struggle between the egocentric desires of childhood and the processes of socialization and maturation. The process is heavily articulated in a discussion amongst the children at the end of the episode in which 'Baby' had been inadvertently propelled into adulthood for a day. The discussion is about socialization, about how to 'improve' Baby so he won't grow up to become the egocentric adult of their adventure, and while the discussion is indecisive in itself, because the processes are beyond childish understanding, it is not difficult to see that the Psammead is a projection of the desired process of socialization, and that the children themselves are unwittingly benefiting from it. And that assumption is the most superior and condescending of any in the book.

'TIME OUT'

I have been suggesting that *Five Children and It* uses the children's 'time out' from the world of adults to show that, in such situations, children are unable to be effectively self-regulating and need to be shaped by adult society in order to be made fit to take their places in it. I want to turn now to three picture books which also represent 'time out' from the framing society, in that the main character of each in some sense runs away from home and from the restrictions and socializing practices represented by the family. The attitude expressed towards that society varies amongst the books from the mildly subversive to the strongly conformist. The three books also share a generic reference, in that the main characters are either animals or wear an animal disguise. Anthropomorphic stories about animals are conventionally used for moral ends in both folk and children's literatures, and their existence as a readily identified genre creates the possibility of carnivalized forms. This possibility is furthered by the use of disguise in two of these books, since disguising is, of course, a common element of carnival. At the same time, though, disguise can be essentially another form of 'time out', the taking on of a different, temporary role or identity which is put off again at the end of the episode. In other words, disguise situates carnival in parentheses.

The earliest of these books is *Harry the Dirty Dog* (story by Gene Zion, pictures by Margaret Bloy Graham), first published in 1956. In this story the socializing practices of the family, specifically focused on the enforced demand for cleanliness, are opposed by the desire for unrestrained play and the physical dirtiness consequent upon it. Thus when Harry hears the tub being filled for his bath, he takes and buries the scrubbing brush and runs away from home. From this point, the first half of the book presents a repetitive sequence rising through intensifed comparatives to a superlative state, then culminating in an apparent change of identity:

> He played where they were mending the street
> > and got very dirty.
> He played by the railway
> > and got even dirtier.
> He played tag with other dogs
> > and became dirtier still.
> He slid down a coal chute
> > and got the dirtiest of all.
> In fact, he changed
> > from a white dog with black spots,
> > to a black dog with white spots.
>
> (Zion, *Harry the Dirty Dog*)

Harry has here reached the crisis point for the carnivalesque hero: having arrived at the point furthest away from the norms of his society, he must examine the consequences of that position, and either attempt to transform 'time out' into permanence, or seek to recuperate the abandoned state. For Harry, the turning-point is when he wonders 'if his family thought that he had *really* run away'. The two key elements here, the formulation 'his family' and the attention to what 'run away' actually signifies, mark the turning back from carnivalesque separation. Moreover, it is at this point that the material body also discloses that its desires are circumscribed by its limitations: 'He felt tired and hungry too.' The role of the family in supplying love and sustenance is perhaps the most significant qualification of the carnivalesque in children's literature and also one of its focal concerns. *Five Children and It* illustrates how food can be used as an instrument of socialization by regulating behaviour through a system of rewards and punishments. One function of carnival is to interrogate this regulatory process, to determine how far love is given conditionally or unconditionally. Thus in *Harry the Dirty Dog* the hero's return is not uncomplicated: despite running back 'without stopping on the way' Harry must still, because of his changed appearance, 'deserve' to be reinstated within the family.

The reinstatement of Harry illustrates one way in which the ambiguous relationship between being a subject and being subjected operates within carnivalesque texts. The last vestige of carnivalesque play occurs in the book with Harry's attempt to prove his identity by performing 'all his old clever tricks', thus situating the familiar within the new circumstance. But this doesn't work, because what is required is the visible Harryness as defined by society (specifically, his pristine state of being a white dog with black spots), which he can only become again by being bathed. That is, he must agree to the demand originally made upon him. Harry, as much as any of the children in *Five Children and It*, is brought to see this for himself and to request it. In this sense the subject is subjected. On the other hand, the ending implicitly has been negotiated, so while it moves to formal closure, with both frame story and inner story resolved together with Harry's return home to be bathed, the element of disclosure – that this is the 'morally' fitting outcome – is qualified by the transgressive implications with which the book ends. Bathed and fed, Harry sleeps 'happily dreaming of how much fun it had been getting dirty. He slept so soundly, he didn't even feel the scrubbing brush he'd hidden under his pillow.'

Harry the Dirty Dog never provoked the kind of controversy sparked by one of our century's great picture books, Maurice Sendak's *Where the Wild Things Are* (1963), probably because the anthropomorphism makes Harry's behaviour amusing rather than threatening, especially since his 'family' is human, not canine (I shall return to this point later, in discussing *Marcella Was Bored*). The child audience can both empathize with Harry's human emotions, especially his desire to play and be dirty, and be distanced from his dogginess. The refusal to be completely socialized is therefore not likely to be construed as a threat to social order. This has not been the case with *Where the Wild Things Are*, and there are several obvious reasons for this. First, Max is human, and his conflict with adult society takes the form of anger and conflict with his mother. Secondly, the disguise motif functions differently and more threateningly here: 'The night Max wore his wolf suit' marks a descent from 'day' and the reasonable and human to 'night' and the irrational and animal, challenging the most basic premises of the socialization process. Further, Max's response to the regulatory 'he was sent to bed without eating anything' is to travel further 'out' until he reaches 'the place where the wild things are' and leads them in 'the wild rumpus'. Much has been written about this book, which brings 'the wild rumpus', the chaos of the animals which rational society fears and holds up as a negative example, into the child's bedroom. The book is in that sense metafictional, since Max's room is the site for the wild rumpus, just as the audience's bedroom is a likely site for the reading of the book. The book has been flagged as a possible source of nightmares, but it is parents who are likely to have them, not children.

Where the Wild Things Are is a carnivalesque text in three important ways: Max's behaviour is oppositional to normal socializing expectations; the 'wild things' in the illustrations are grotesques, and thus in essence parodies of the natural creatures usually encountered during a wilderness adventure; and the book clearly belongs to the 'time out' group, in that Max's adventure is formally a parenthesis in his relationship with his mother. Roger H. Ford (1979) has suggested that the main characters in several of Sendak's books are modelled on the folk-tale Trickster figure, dominated by selfish appetites and emotions, given to practical jokes, capable of heroism, and generally unselfconscious. Max's entry into the land of the wild things, whether we regard it as a dream or an act of the imagination, enables him to enjoy a time of unconcerned spontaneity free of the social constraints which define his behaviour in the world as 'mischief'. Max's attempt to construct a site for fantasy play in the opening illustration involves causing damage to property, as is foregrounded by the grossly oversized hammer with which he attempts to drive a huge nail into the wall. His second act of mischief is to attack the family dog with a kitchen fork, an actual breach of proper conduct going beyond the quasi-'hanging' of his teddy bear included in the first illustration. Max, then, still deeply immersed in the solipsism of childhood, has not yet learnt the first principle of freedom – that freedom of action is bounded by the rights of others. Carnivalesque texts, by breaching those boundaries, explore where they properly lie and the ideological bases for their determination, but without always necessarily redrawing those boundaries.

The grotesque functions to bring down to earth all that is high and idealized, to give bodily form to the mysterious. If life is to be seen as a process of shaping, growth and becoming, the grotesque acts as a reminder that this *is* a process, and that reason and order are socially constructed ideals which can be regarded with a proper ambivalence. Bakhtin (1984, p. 62) argues that the grotesque is part of a double-faceted process which both affirms the material and bodily and is a phase in the development of something new and better. I want to argue below that this is the case with *Where the Wild Things Are*, in that the story achieves closure with Max's 'return' and the giving and receiving of food, but also implies a growth in the parent–child relationship. The grotesque in the book is comic and droll, rather than frightening, though this was not always perceived when the book was first published. And yet this is important, since one way in which the book invites to be read is as a coming to terms with the potential wildness of one's own inner being. By giving comically grotesque forms to inner fears, the illustrations image the defeat of that fear. Moreover, Max is always in control. Swanton (1971) offers this as one reason why children do not find the book frightening. Nodelman (1988, p. 127) also suggests that a cultural assumption we make is that rounded shapes are accommodating, and since the Wild Things are all comfortably round, as distinct from Max's own jagged edges, the illustrations in this way suggest the child has little to fear from the monsters.

Finally, as remarked earlier, Max's adventure constitutes a period of 'time out' in his relationship with his mother. It is his mother who introduces the concept 'wild thing' to the story in one of only two brief pieces of conversation in the book:

[1]   his mother called him 'WILD THING!'
[2]   and Max said 'I'LL EAT YOU UP!'
[3]   so he was sent to bed without eating anything.

(Sendak, *Where the Wild Things Are*)

Questions of authority and domination arise here in the slippage of meaning from line to line and the demands made on the audience to infer appropriate implicatures retrospectively. Thus the action described in the third line suggests that a disapproving view has been taken towards the sentiment expressed in the second, and so the action consequently defines that sentiment as {+aggressive} and {+rebellious} rather than {+playful}. The exchange in lines 1–2 is thus redefined as a stronger struggle for conversational dominance than it would seem to be on the surface, especially if the mother's 'wild thing' were understood as playful. This takes us two ways: one, into the indeterminacies of affection and authority in parent–child relationships, and two, into the ambiguous spirit of carnival, with its blurring of the serious and the comic. Max explores the former through the latter, using the transposed hierarchies of carnival to act out parental roles for himself. Having tamed the wild things and been made their king, Max ordains 'the wild rumpus', illustrated in three, wordless, double-page spreads, only to call a halt with: '"Now stop!" Max said and sent the wild things off to bed without their supper.' But this parody of exercising the parent's seemingly arbitrary power, of being 'king of all wild things', exposes the emptiness of power without love, so 'lonely' Max 'wanted to be where someone loved him best of all'. The slight indeterminacy of 'best of all' (either 'more than anyone else', or as an idiomatic compound intensifying the verb) is felicitous here, displacing power with love. The first conversation is then recast in the book's second exchange, when Max bids farewell to the wild things, and in which the conjunction of belonging, 'eating' and loving is explicitly articulated:

> But the wild things cried, 'Oh please don't go –
> we'll eat you up – we love you so!'
> And Max said, 'No!'
>
> (Sendak, *Where the Wild Things Are*)

In this way, the carnivalesque has been used not to question the values of the official world but to define the values which may be at most implicit in some of the puzzling actions performed by those in power. In this respect, it is important to see that Max's return and his mother's gift of 'supper' are not causally linked but contiguous, since each is unconditional. This seems to me a far more imaginatively and emotionally satisfying way to examine the question of power in parent–child relations than the explicit and heavy-handed approach of Nesbit.

This is not a claim that we necessarily do things better now. Robert Byrd's *Marcella Was Bored* (1986) shows that a version of the theme explored in *Harry the Dirty Dog* and *Where the Wild Things Are* can still be quite heavy-handed. This is a book aimed at an affluent, middle-class audience, teaching that a little temporary deprivation might make children better appreciate how well-off they are. While the book has the structure of a 'time out' carnivalesque, it lacks the interrogative effect because Marcella's boredom is a self-inflicted state of mind and her cure means conforming enthusiastically with the social activities she finds so boring at the beginning of the book. Her time in the 'wilderness', unlike Harry's or Max's, offers no comment on the significance of the everyday. The text, and especially the illustrations, make it clear that her boredom is an incorrect response to her situation. For example, half the text accompanying the second illustration, a double-page spread crammed with siblings, books, games, and so on, reads:

> She looked through her new monster book.
> 'Monsters are so boring,' Marcella declared. 'Besides, it's too noisy in here to read.'
>
> (Byrd, *Marcella Was Bored*)

There are three indicators of Marcella's error here. The collocation <'new' + 'monster book'> reflects the assumption that both novelty and difference are intrinsically interesting; more directly, Marcella's lack of interest is bound to earn her the scorn of most child audiences. Secondly, the *inquit*-tag 'declared' almost invariably has a pejorative association in children's books, marking an utterance as opiniated or wrong, and thus reinforces the audience's sense of her error. And her second sentence – 'it's too noisy . . .' – indicates her determination to find fault with everything. The important factor in all of this, however, is that in distancing readers from Marcella the text creates an implicit subject position for readers which is identical with the middle class ideology and values which form the basis for criticism of the character here, and which she embraces at the end. In this regard, too, it is also significant that Marcella, her family and her friends are all heavily anthropomorphic cats. The only activities which are not human are the grandfather's allusions to encounters with mice and dogs. To the normal distancing effect of picture-book format is thus added the additional factor that the empathy encouraged by anthropomorphism is blocked by the character's 'deviant' behaviour. The book thus assumes the truth value of the moral it seeks to inculcate.

Comparison with *Where the Wild Things Are*, which might well qualify as a 'monster book', seems inevitable, and in some ways *Marcella Was Bored* seems to invite being read as a corrective to Sendak's book: the allusion to monsters, the contrastive verb tenses of the two titles ('are'/'was'), and the journey into the 'wilderness'. In the wilderness, however, Marcella meets no monsters, but bees, frogs and crows, which are either hostile (when provoked), or indifferent to her, and she does find food. The elements of Sendak's book which are so stimulating to the imagination here seem to be systematically re-encoded as signs which point to things in the most direct possible way in order to produce the *one* significance: that good, middle-class children should assiduously devote themselves to the activities of their comfortable, material world. One of the functions of carnival is, through the dialectic of high and low, to affirm the temporal and material against the higher claims of the eternal and transcendent, but this is a gross materialism which allows no possibility of any dialectic. The playful and the ambivalence of the grotesque have been elided and replaced with a wholeness of being which is small and comfortable, contained within a text which tends towards a single meaning and a uniformly serious tone.

INVERTING IDEOLOGICAL PARADIGMS

The two books which I have chosen to illustrate the second type of interrogative text, the text which examines and inverts a social ideological paradigm, are versions of the 'male cinderella' theme. This is more obvious with Babette Cole's *Prince Cinders*, which quickly reveals that it is a playful re-version of *Cinderella*, and so just as quickly draws attention to itself as a *text* at three removes from the 'original': it is a retelling; the sex of the main character has been changed; and the language is contemporary, idiomatic and parodic. Anthony Browne's *Willy the Wimp* has its narrative origins (though not its format) rather in comic book fantasy transformations, but also draws attention to its own textuality by visual and verbal quotation, and other devices such as a clenched fist bursting through the centre of the title page (which in effect declares that 'this is *not* a clenched fist bursting through . . .').

The Cinderella story has rich possibilities for carnivalization. Its fundamental assertion is that the subject is constituted in social roles and social perception: the main character is a classic example of such a construction of subjectivity, since she is always defined by her appearance and roles, deprived of individual subjectivity, and subjected to the wills and actions of others (step-family, godmother, prince). Ideologically, she represents a model of perfect wifehood – she is beautiful but abject, and she is available but submissive, in that the slipper symbolizes her sexual aptness and her passivity, 'fitting' but waiting to be found. At the end of her story her virtues are recognized and rewarded.

When a male figure replaces Cinderella, the ideological bearings of the story are immediately scrambled and interrogated. That abjection, humility and passivity now become deficiencies poses the question of why they should be virtues for the female; what constitutes desirable traits in a male in such a situation likewise reminds us that what is socially desirable and socially undesirable are cultural and linguistic constructs. Both picture books make effective use of the grotesque in doing this, for both suggest that, in constructing masculinity and femininity oppositionally, our society has idealized what is grotesque in masculine appearance and behaviour.

Prince Cinders inverts the story of Cinderella almost point by point. I want now to consider four motifs as they appear in the text to illustrate how it functions interrogatively, and to do so will make some comparisons with Fiona French's *Cinderella*, also published in 1987. I have chosen the latter because it represents the kind of minimal picture-book text which is an appropriate intertext for *Prince Cinders*, it is traditional in its grotesque representation of the step-sisters, and it contains no obvious traces of humour or irony. It thus also shows that the story's ideological paradigm is still being reproduced. I begin with the opening sentences.

(1)   Once there was a gentleman who married a proud and haughty lady for his second wife.
      She had two daughters who were just like her.
      After the wedding he brought them home to meet his own daughter, who was a beautiful, sweet girl.
      The new step-mother could not bear to see her beauty beside her own plain daughters.
      So she put her to work in the kitchen, washing the dishes, scrubbing the floors, and raking out the cinders in the fireplace.

(French, *Cinderella*)

(2)   Prince Cinders was not much of a prince.
      He was small, spotty, scruffy and skinny.
      He had three big hairy brothers who were always teasing him
      about his looks.
      They spent their time going to the Palace Disco with Princess girl-
      friends.
      They made poor Prince Cinders stay behind and clean up after
      them.

(Cole, *Prince Cinders*)

While French's language is not particularly complex, it does establish an identifiable 'fairy-story' register. It uses the traditional
opening signals, the temporal 'Once' beginning an impersonal
clause; it makes apt lexical choices in 'gentleman' and 'lady', in the
doublet 'proud and haughty', and in the repetition of 'beauti-
ful/beauty'; and its syntax seems formal, especially because of the
parallel *who*-clauses in the first three sentences. In addition, it in-
stantly establishes the kind of binary opposition expected in a fairy
story – 'proud and haughty' against 'beautiful, sweet'. Cole's language is the obverse of this. The first sentence indicates the process
in that, beginning and ending with 'prince', it introduces an inap-
propriate register by placing the idiomatic 'not much of a' in
between, and sustains this register into the qualifiers of sentence
two, especially the colloquial 'spotty, scruffy'. These qualifiers are
also part of two key oppositions here:

[small, spotty, scruffy and skinny
  big hairy

[They spent their time going . . .
  They made poor Prince Cinders stay behind . . .

The second is basic to the story, whereas the first is basic to the
theme: what constitutes masculine desirability? Unlike *Cinderella*,
however, it is not clear that the opposition privileges one side, especially since the accompanying illustration represents the brothers as
grotesque parodies, with moustaches, five-o'clock shadows, and
heavy gold chains on hairy chests. Devotees of Cole's books will
also recognize in this representation a reminiscence of her earlier
foray into the grotesquery of hairiness in *The Hairy Book* (1984). It
may well be that many male children will still accept the following
paradigm:

Good	Bad
big	small
	skinny
hairy	spotty
	scruffy

Cole, however, sets out to destroy it. In a hilarious parody of the Cinderella story, Cinders' helper is 'a dirty fairy [who] fell down the chimney' wearing a school uniform. Her effort to fit Cinders for the Disco goes awry at each step, because fairy magic depends on a particular kind of relationship between words and things, and Cinders' fairy finds the relationship is both too close and uncontrollable. When the godmother in French's *Cinderella* works her magic, 'At once her rags became a beautiful gown of gold and silver, and on her feet were two glass slippers'. But when Cinders' fairy tries to dress him in a 'suit' and to grant his wish to be 'big and hairy', she does so by transforming him into a large ape wearing a swim suit. It is as if Cinderella became a grotesque like one of her step-sisters. Bakhtin (p. 48) remarks that fairy-tale worlds are strange, but they are not worlds that have *become* alienated in the way that Cinders' transformation alienates him increasingly from his own subjectivity. When grotesque elements are introduced, the familiar is not only transformed but also may become threatening, both to the self as subject and to others. Most tellingly (see Plate 4), 'Prince Cinders didn't know he was a big hairy monkey because that's the kind of spell it was. He thought he looked pretty good!' (Cole, *Prince Cinders*). In the illustration, Cinders 'sees' himself as looking like one of his brothers. As ape gazes into mirror, and prince gazes back, the interplay of representations dismantles that whole image of masculinity; as Cinders becomes subjected to cultural and linguistic illusions, ensnared in a masculine paradigm, the reader is offered a subject position from which to view the operation of that paradigm and to see it as a constructed illusion.

Cinders doesn't make it to the Disco (he's too big to get inside), but instead has an important encounter at a bus stop, at the stroke of midnight, with Princess Lovelypenny. Terrified by Cinders-as-ape, she assumes that the disenchanted Cinders has saved her, but he flees, leaving behind his trousers. The significance of all this hardly needs spelling out. The very carnivalesque touch of the lost trousers, comic in itself, is also an example of how sexuality in children's literature is generally displaced into the removal of cloth-

Prince Cinders didn't know he was a big hairy monkey because that's the kind of spell it was.

He thought he looked pretty good!

Plate 4   *Prince Cinders*

ing, so there is the double effect here of enabling the bridegroom to be selected on the basis of fitting Cinders' trousers, and the comic inversion of 'every prince for miles around' standing about in variously patterned boxer shorts. The move also begins to demystify sex. It would be too heavy-handed to explain that the slipper symbolizes the vagina (as it does), but Cole carnivalizes the motif by substituting Cinders' trousers instead. And of course his big hairy brothers have no hope of fitting inside his diminutive trousers. If Cinderella is the perfect sexual partner because the shoe fits, so is Cinders because the trousers fit, and he and the Princess 'lived in luxury, happily ever after'.

Cole then pursues her theme to its end in the motif of the subsequent treatment of the unkind siblings, in a closure which is a powerful thematic disclosure indeed. Cinderella 'kissed her sisters and forgave them all their cruelty' (French), but Lovelypenny issues instructions to Cinders' fairy, who 'turned [the big hairy brothers] into house fairies. And they flitted around the palace doing the housework for ever and ever'. There is more to this than a motif of revenge, which, significantly, is absent from versions of 'Cinderella' derived from Perrault. Rather, I think, by this final inversion of the story Cole is making the 'big hairy' image utterly ridiculous and finally unrecuperable.

Willy the Wimp is also a playful carnivalizing of a traditional narrative in order to interrogate and invert a paradigm of masculinity. It uses characters which are very anthropomorphic gorillas in order to examine a comic book version of a masculinity fantasy. As a point of interest, the crucial term *wimp* is itself probably derived from the comic-book sub-culture, namely from the cowardly Mr Wimpy who appears in *Popeye* comics. The narrative models drawn on in *Willy the Wimp*, and explicitly articulated on facing pages, are, first, the Superman story, in which wimpish Clark Kent becomes transformed into invincible Superman (or, in this case, Supergorilla), and second, the familiar comic-book advertisements for body-building courses and devices which promise to transform harmless wimps into aggressive MEN. As a fantasy, the story is actually structured as an inverted 'time out' carnivalesque, in the sense that Willy's meek personality, which frames the book, represents his real subjectivity, and his growth into a hero figure is a process of temporary subjection to a false paradigm. An illustration showing Willy at a body-building club, for example (Plate 5), makes clever use of the text's anthropomorphism. Standing knock-kneed in the centre front of the picture, tiny Willy is framed by two huge gorillas holding conventional body-builder poses and whose bodies are 'human' not simian. Once again, at the heart of the book lies a sense that the relationship between signs and things is not only arbitrary but also socially determined. Willy is a 'wimp' because 'The suburban gorillas *called* him Willy the Wimp' (my emphasis). In the body-building picture, the mingling of the pictorial signs for 'gorilla' and 'human' serve to evoke the main verbal signifieds for *gorilla*: 'the largest of the anthropoid apes' and 'an ugly, brutal person'. The double meaning is earlier more overtly present in the description of how 'the suburban gorilla gang bullied [Willy]', where 'gorilla' is drawn into the same semantic field as 'gang' and 'bullied'.

The dichotomy between the signifieds of *gorilla* and *human* is already present in Browne's parodic version of the advertisement. It begins by offering, in highly emotive language, to transpose roles of aggression and submission:

Plate 5   *Willy the Wimp*

I *was* a scrawny, skinny-chested
pathetic weakling. NOW
I can order people about
kick sand in THEIR faces.

(Browne, *Willy the Wimp*)

The parodic irony here is obvious, but is complicated both linguistically and conceptually at the end of the advertisement:

Do YOU want
Bulging arm muscles
Tireless legs
A deep chest
A large wardrobe
A magnetic personality?

(Browne, *Willy the Wimp*)

The shift into verbal jokiness with the play of signifiers in 'deep/large' and 'chest/wardrobe' implies how comically absurd is the preceding stretch, and points not just to the irrelevance of the conclusion but to the cultural error in confusing aggression with attractiveness to others. The book's closure/disclosure presents this significance in yet another way. The scene in which the 'new', transformed Willy saves Millie from the suburban gorillas has a double climax. First is a conversation, if it can be called that, which parodies the conventional romantic outcome of the masculinity fantasy:

> 'Oh . . . Willy,' said Millie.
> 'What, Millie?' said Willy.
> 'You're my hero, Willy,' said Millie.
> 'Oh . . . Millie,' said Willy.
>
> (Browne, *Willy the Wimp*)

The lack of content and general inarticulateness, foregrounded by the constant repetition of the nearly alike names in both speeches and *inquit*-tags, functions as a gentle mockery of the idea that physical attributes translate into personality attributes, and foreshadows the final deconstruction of the masculinity fantasy in the second, and ultimate, climax. This is presented in a set of four frames over a double page, becoming very reminiscent of a conventional comic-book sequence in which pride meets a fall. It runs as follows:

> [1]   Willy was proud. [*in profile, head high, shoulders back*]
> [2]   'I'm not a wimp!' [*head higher, eyes closed, drawn larger*]
> [3]   A hero. [*head turned, eyes still closed, grinning full front at reader*]
> [4]   BANG! [*drawn smaller again, collides with lamp-post*]
>
> (Browne, *Willy the Wimp*)

The third frame is an interesting example of how subject positions can be manipulated. The closed eyes prevent direct eye contact between character and reader, so the reader is pushed more firmly into an observer role than the mere representation of the character in profile would effect. Sympathy is being withdrawn from Willy, so the quite literal deflation which takes place on the final page – a return to the 'wimpy' figure who apologizes to inanimate objects –

can function more efficiently as a deflation of the whole ideological paradigm.

TRANSGRESSING PARADIGMS OF AUTHORITY

The final type of interrogative text consists of a small group of works which are endemically transgressive of such things as social authority, received paradigms of behaviour and morality, and major literary genres. Books which radically transgress against authority – whether parental, educational, or state – tend to be treated with suspicion by those who mediate between texts and their audience. It is not my intention to suggest that such suspicion is always unwarranted, though perhaps its basis in particular notions of social order and structure needs to be acknowledged. The long-term mixed reaction to the writings of Robert Cormier affords a well-known example, in that Cormier is sometimes accused of attempting to undermine the confidence of his readers in the legitimacy of state and educational apparatuses. I am not going to concern myself with Cormier here, however, both because he writes for an audience older than that with which I am concerned, and because I do not find that his works employ any sustained carnivalesque strategies. They are rather wedded to the illusion-making of 'new realism'.

Instead, I intend to examine two works by English writers which seem to me to be, in different ways, good examples of carnivalesque interrogative texts. The first, *Out of the Oven* by Jan Mark and Antony Maitland, deals narratively with the abstract notions of good and evil, playfully deconstructing the conventional organization into opposition and hierarchy. Mark has explored the possibilities of carnivalesque texts quite extensively in other works, notably in short stories such as 'Frankie's Hat', 'Chutzpah', and 'Send Three-and-fourpence, We Are Going to a Dance'. The second example is Jan Needle's *Wagstaffe the Wind-up Boy* (henceforth *Wagstaffe*), a book which, its narrator reassures us, does not set out to be 'a naice book, that got awards and was put in the library by naice ladies who thought it was a naice read for naice boys and girlies' (p. 65). Rather, it is a jokey, tricksy, abrasive book that challenges the way society expects children to think about a range of social structures: the family, school, literature, the entertainment industry, big business. Needle's books disclose a high level of socio-political commitment, and in any one of them he is apt to situate the individual's existential freedom against a broad range of constraining ideological social apparatuses. As a writing strategy, Needle employs the carnivalesque pervasively in his books for younger readers – especially, apart from *Wagstaffe*, in *The Size Spies* and *Wild Wood* (*The Wind in the Willows* retold from the working-class point of view of Baxter the ferret). It appears elsewhere in *Behind the Bike Sheds*, for example, but Needle's books for older readers, such as *A Pitiful Place* or *A Sense of Shame*, incline more towards what Julia Kristeva (1982, pp. 140–1) has identified as 'abject' literature ('the sort that takes up where apocalypse and carnival left off'), dealing with the theme of suffering–horror. Again, my concern here is not with such books for older readers.

In what ways is Mark and Maitland's *Out of the Oven* a transgressive text? This picture book finds verbal and visual representations of good and evil by making the familiar strange and by overturning some conventional aspects of picture book mode, and in so doing subverts family authority and both ecclesiastical and academic wisdom. The story originates in a prohibition expressed as a folk-idiom, when Matty's grandmother forbids Matty to open the oven door 'or the devils will get out', though it is in fact Gran herself who breaches the prohibition, releasing a devil in the shape of a black kitten. This book is yet another variation on the picture book convention of treating animals anthropomorphically; here, text and illustration interact so that the devil both is, and is not, a cat, whereas the ordinary cats in the book are always represented as cats. When Matty first finds the devil, for example, the text describes him as if he were a lost kitten: 'when he saw that the others had gone without him he put out his claws, as fine as white eyelashes, and cried like a kitten, *meeow meeow*', but the illustration represents him as humanoid, sitting upright with rear legs crossed and wringing his front paws together. Henceforth, the devil's limbs and body postures are consistently humanoid. The devil not only refuses to conform to the behaviour of a picture-book cat, however, but is also the object which most frequently protrudes beyond the slightly ornate frames which Maitland places around many of his illustrations. Perhaps the most notable example occurs when the text explains how the devil began going to church every Sunday (Plate 6). Here, looking his most cat-like, the devil is placed almost entirely outside the frame from where he watches people entering the church; the frame is also broken by the top of the church tower, which apparently reaches towards Heaven. The two breaches relate antithetically, and make a line which slices diagonally across the picture. The strategic placement of the cat emphasizes that he is an outsider at the point at which he is about to extend his subversive career by reproducing.

"You can't put him back in the oven now," Matty said to Gran, when they got home. "Not after he's been to church."

The little devil remembered the grating where the warm air comes up, and he went to church every Sunday, after that. No more was said about putting him back in the oven.

Plate 6   *Out of the Oven*

Although Matty is not originally responsible for releasing the devil from the oven, once it is out she resists all suggestions that it should be put back, and the devil gradually comes to represent the child's own impulses to resist and subvert the authoritative structures of official society. The insistence here on the literal meaning of a metaphorical idiom is an immediate example of how the relationship between words and things is harnessed as a particular contribution to the carnivalesque quality of this book. Matty's naming practice, for example, is designed to assert 'catness' in the face of her pet's evident devilishness: hence with the original devil, 'Matty called him Tiddles, and hoped that Gran would forget he was a little devil', and with the first of his diabolical offspring, ' "Now we have another little devil," said Matty. She called him Puss, so that no one should guess.' That is, the child has learned that there is scope for duplicity within apparent conformity. Further, her response to her Gran's conforming 'I can't keep a lumping great devil in my house. What would the vicar say?' is to take the devil to church and assert its catness. The disabling of the vicar is achieved by means of the same linguistic assertiveness:

> 'That's a fine figure of a cat you have there,' the vicar said, after the service.
> 'Thank you, sir,' said Matty.
> The vicar stroked the little devil between the ears and looked surprised.
> 'Are you sure it's a cat?' said the vicar.
> 'He's called Tiddles,' said Matty.
> 'Well, he's certainly a . . . fine figure of a cat,' said the vicar.
> (Mark and Maitland, *Out of the Oven*)

One of the ways in which children are socially disempowered is in the operation of conversational exchange. Here, Matty is seen to take control of the conversation by deftly breaching the Gricean maxim of relation in her reply to the vicar's question. She does not tell an outright lie, but the implicated response – Tiddle's is a cat's name, therefore Tiddle's is a cat – has to be inferred from her reply, and because it is not explicit it apparently leaves the vicar nowhere to go but back to his original statement. Matty's pretended innocence opens the way for a carnivalesque intrusion of diablerie into institutional religion. When the devil was in the church he 'sat on the grating where the warm air comes up and said "Meeow meeow," when everyone else said, "Amen amen"'. The suggestion here is that the devil uses its catness to make a response which is in fact oppositional. Further, the impunity with which Tiddles and his descendants occupy the church suggests that there is no power there that can exclude them. The investigation of the cat–devil phenomenon by 'scholars and other learned persons' founders on this, encapsulated in a point of (il)logic of the same order which has asserted the devils' catness:

'Are you sure these are cats? . . .'
'They catch mice, don't they?'

'They look more like little devils to me'
'Whoever heard of devils going to church?'

(Mark and Maitland, *Out of the Oven*)

That this carnivalesque diablerie remains uncontained by official culture is shown by the book's final page. The illustration pictures five devil–cats within a frame shaped like a squashed Gothic window. They are bathed in rainbow light, and three of them protrude outside the frame. The text reads:

The little devils sat in a row on the grating and purred devoutly, louder than the organ and sweeter than the choir. The sun shone clear through a stained-glass saint, and gilded their horns.

(Mark and Maitland, *Out of the Oven*)

The set of oppositions here spell out the empowerment of the devils. Not only are they superior to organ and choir, but they appropriate the attributes of the other – devoutness, and especially light. The saint's lack of opacity is a final gesture of the helplessness of an institution unable to resist penetration by antithetical values. Indeed, in so far as the sunlight transfers colour from the stained-glass saint to the devils' horns, the conclusion offers a parodic version of the power of a socially constructed 'good' to throw light, here literally, on what is constructed as evil. Through this relativizing of 'evil', the book offers a strong sense of how the power of social institutions can be restructured by the carnivalizing spirit.

Jan Needle's *Wagstaffe* does not propose any restructuring of social institutions. Rather, the main character's own material body functions as a figure for contemporary society: unwanted, unclean, disorderly, addicted to mayhem, unloved and unlovable, it is anarchically destroyed and arbitrarily remade. Wagstaffe moves from the subordinated role of child in a nuclear family to the limited freedom of living independently but with a large key in the middle of his back which he cannot always wind for himself. From there, he has to discover how to live within society without destroying it or being destroyed.

Of all the books discussed in this chapter, *Wagstaffe* most overtly flaunts its textuality in order to preclude reader empathy. The book may begin as an apparently straightforward realistic narrative – 'This is the story of a boy called Wagstaffe. He was a very ordinary boy in many ways . . .' – but it quickly reveals itself as a parody of an adventure story, told by an intrusive narrator who poses questions for the reader and gives the reader mock advice and instruction, operating within the kind of comic narrative mode available to the novel since *Tristram Shandy*. It is a carnivalesque mode, replete with grotesquery and both breaking the fictive illusion in a number of ways and permitting apparently contradictory positions which disclose much social 'morality' as hypocrisy. For example, although the book uses a register which falls within the milder end of the taboo spectrum, and is thus calculated to shock, it incorporates both an 'official' and a carnivalesque attitude towards this language. One of Wagstaffe's early unpleasant experiences concludes,

> The man had said something very rude. Much too rude to put in a book for children. Wagstaffe had done it.
>
> (Needle, *Wagstaffe the Wind-up Boy*, p. 11)

The third sentence uses inferencing to undermine the apparent reticence of the second, on the pattern by which children themselves will introduce taboo words by hints and indirection. That is, it is suggested that it is hypocritical to evoke the *thing* but avoid its *name*. For children, taboo language can be baffling because it interdicts some signifiers but not others for the same signified, and its interdiction seems totally arbitrary and not applicable to adults. Taboo language forms part of an awful parody of the process of socialization applied to Wagstaffe. At first his mother 'tried to turn him into a Proper Little Boy. First it was How to Wash. Then it was How to Dress. Then it was How to Behave . . .' and so on (p. 28). But his parents then resorted to ridicule and began to call him names, beginning with 'Smelly Bum' (p. 29). Wagstaffe, of course, was not allowed to reciprocate:

> One day his father said to him: 'How are you this morning, disgusting little blob of sicked up maggot's food?'
> Wagstaffe replied: 'Not bad thank you, Fatguts Stinkbreath. And yourself?'
> To Wagstaffe, it seemed a not bad thing to say. His father was fat. He

could hide a cream cake in his belly button. And his breath smelled like long dead cheese.
    His father hit him.

(Needle, Wagstaffe the Wind-up Boy, p. 32)

The incident exaggerates the kind of unequal power relationship which underlies adult–child conversational exchanges. Its pragmatic frame and register are those of a polite exchange, though those elements are perhaps too formal for a morning greeting; the elaborated, abusive terms of address, however, transform this into a paradox of politeness, whereby Wagstaffe, the second speaker, appears not merely to be observing the co-operative principle of manner, by responding in the same register, but to be making an attempt to assume conversational dominance by superimposing the principle of quality, in that he replies to what is not literally true ('blob of sicked up maggot's food') with something that is arguably true, as the subsequent explanation indicates. The incident is thus more than a carnivalesque use of taboo language in order to shock or titillate. It is also a serious comment on how control over language is used in adult–child conversations to inculcate and maintain a particular structure of dominance.

Matters of naming are important in the book, especially in the early chapters, and form a central part of the wider issue of *name–thing* relationships. They also link with other questions, such as 'What is Literature?' and how is this determined. Needle brings these together in Chapter 8, a Shandyesque discourse on the name 'Smelly Bum'. Beginning with the premise 'His bum did smell', the narrator pursues a logical chain to demonstrate both that name and thing were aptly related and that, while Wagstaffe liked his smell, it was not entirely his fault but was imposed upon him by social causality: he was not allowed to use the bathroom. This logical chain, however, is itself deconstructed at the end of the chapter through one of the book's overt self-reflexive moments:

> Have you noticed something about this chapter? All but seven of the paragraphs start with the word The, and all but nine with the phrase The Reason. This means that it is LITERATURE. Ask your teacher. Now let's have some more rude names.

(Needle, Wagstaffe the Wind-up Boy, pp. 29–30)

Literature is thus orderly and rhetorical, and can be discussed by counting unimportant items and disregarding content. Ask your teacher. Literature as it is officially constituted institutionalizes a divorce between signs and things. The aim of the interrogative text is to focus attention back not just on the relationship of sign to thing but on the social forces which determine what that relationship will be. One way to do this is to turn from the play of signifiers to an unacceptable register, 'some more rude names'. The game doesn't end there, however, for it seems that teacher (and/or narrator, for that matter) cannot count. The chapter only has seven paragraphs, with six beginning with 'The' and five with 'The reason'. The comment apes the meaninglessness it describes, before turning from official Literature to its carnivalesque inversion.

This self-consciousness about the nature of the text itself has much wider ramifications. While *Wagstaffe* does tell a story, it is not a book which offers an easily accessible 'reading'. Indeed it resists that. Its story is overall a parody of the fantasy adventure in which children rescue their parents from danger or death, exploiting its overt unreality and textuality to interrogate that whole genre. It also embeds other story motifs such as the science-fiction 'bionic man' and the fantasy of running away to join a circus (except it is the parents, not the child, who do this). The conventional frame story-pattern is overtly mocked, as when, for example, it is Wagstaffe who draws attention to the ironical link between his parents' imminently fatal attempt to go over Niagara Falls in a pedalo and the time his father sent Wagstaffe off in a pedalo to attempt to circumnavigate the Isle of Wight. Or again, when he swims up to his parents on 'the brink of doom' and addresses them in best British hero register – 'Come on . . . Chins up . . . Aren't you pleased to see me?' – his mother finally responds, 'You haven't got the brains you were born with, have you? Why don't you stop talking rubbish and save our lives?' (p. 148).

Further, for much of the book it is difficult to like Wagstaffe, even though he is the only character whose mind the narrator enters and who acts as a focalizer. He is personally and physically unattractive, totally solipsistic, ill-mannered, not individualistic, dishonest, ungrateful and pointlessly aggressive and destructive. He does, however, become less solipsistic later in the book, and even becomes quite likeable and invites some empathy, though this is still somewhat offset by reminders that he is 'half clockwork'. The ways in which the character is represented and the changes he undergoes are significant thematically and ideologically. His early problems with his names and his material body, on the one hand, and his dislikeable personality, on the other, had functioned oppositionally to call in question the idea of an autonomous subjective identity. His subjectivity thus becomes a product of his destructive and constructive relationships with society: his early personality being formed under his parents' mishandling; his body, and consequently his personality, being reshaped by the benign Dr Dhondy, and by his only other real helper, Mandy Badsox: two people who offer models of genuine, disinterested concern for another. The result is a shift from moral anarchy to an interrogation of social values leading to a growth into a capacity for unconditional concern for others, fuelled by a developing ability to make moral discriminations which seems sadly lacking in surrounding society. Wagstaffe is a grotesque, both before and after his accident, but the real grotesque is a society in which a body can lie unattended by a roadside, or in which thousands of people will spend 'good money to watch some sucker die' (p. 158).

The effect of the various forms of textual self-consciousness is to construct a complex subject position for the reader. The grotesque language and behaviour and the (at times) anarchic narrative processes construct a position which is sometimes quite close to that implied for the narrator, and sometimes, especially towards the end of the book, close to Wagstaffe as he shifts from a subjected subject to an active subjective identity able to interrogate the flaws and motives of the world and his own relationship to it.

Wagstaffe does not end romantically. It has a formal story closure, in which Wagstaffe saves his parents, the villain dies in their stead, and the family returns to England, where Wagstaffe expects that Dr Dhondy will again reconstruct his now dilapidated body. But Wagstaffe's parents are unchanged by their experiences and are locked as tightly as ever within their myopic egocentricity. The disclosure is contained by the limited optimism that can be derived from Mandy's last words to Wagstaffe: 'You can trust me . . . And Dr Dhondy sounds all right. But apart from that . . .'. The world is chaotic and meaningless in itself; it can't be saved, nor substantially changed, but it can be understood and endured by reaching out.

CONCLUSION

The three kinds of carnivalesque interrogative text examined here illustrate some special uses of intertextuality. Subject positions in such texts are less constrained than in most other kinds of text, and this is most apparent where textual strategies are used which, undermining the illusion of fictionality, draw attention to textuality itself. Such strategies are in turn most apparent where the narrator is playfully intrusive, or where linguistic playfulness is directed towards a problematizing of the world's serious, but unthinking, acceptance of unconditional meanings, social structures and ideological paradigms.

The principal effect of the interrogative text is to foreground the processes of signification whereby signs are related to things, and thence to draw attention to the social forces which determine what that relationship will be. Readers are thus constantly reminded that what is socially desirable and socially undesirable are cultural and linguistic constructs. By making the familiar strange and by overturning some conventional aspects of narrative and picture book modes, these books are able to see the world differently, less seriously, and to question and sometimes subvert a variety of its ideologies and structures of authority. Major characters may speak or behave in a manner oppositional to normal socializing expectations, or the ideological basis of conformist behaviour is examined in order to confirm or reject that behaviour. The books do not advocate anarchic disobedience, for example, but they do recognize that adult authority *is* often arbitrary, that its exercise is often arbitrary, and that it is often merely a veneer covering radical incompetence.

The most notable effect of these strategies is to discourage unquestioning empathy or identification with the main characters as subjects and to situate the reader as a separately constructed subject firmly outside the text, sometimes as a subject position in opposition to society's official structures of authority.

TAKING IT FURTHER

Carnivalesque elements may be investigated in various kinds of texts only briefly mentioned or not examined here. Books depicting children at play may be carnivalesque, though not necessarily interrogative. The 'Hungry Three' picture books by Russell Hoban and Colin McNaughton are a good example, raising such questions as: how do children reallocate object functions and linguistic signs in imaginative play? Does remaking the world through play question adult constructions of reality? How do adults (that is, 'official culture') co-operate with but also contain children's play? Perhaps the most interesting books to consider are Hoban and McNaughtons' *The Great Fruitgum Robbery* and *They Came From Aargh!* (1982).

A number of fictional sub-genres can be appropriated for interrogative effect. The 'school story' has an inherent or potential conflict between the subjectivity of children and the authority of adults. In *Hairs in the Palm of the Hand* (1981) Jan Mark pairs two long, contrasting school stories: in 'Time and the Hour', a class's attempt to carnivalize their school-time is neatly captured and controlled by their teachers; in 'Chutzpah', the main character uses 'time out' carnival to wreak havoc on the first day back at school. Carnivalesque elements have an interesting place in Gene Kemp's *The Turbulent Term of Tyke Tyler* (1977) and in John Burningham's *John Patrick Norman McHennessy – the boy who was always late* (1987).

Tales of the supernatural, of outlaws, pirates, and the like, which may be grounded in alternative realities or altered moral frames, are always potentially carnivalesque and/or interrogative, and can be profitably explored. A comparison of, for example, Barbara Willard's *Spell Me a Witch* (1979) and Diana Wynne Jones's *Witch Week* (1982) will raise questions about alternative societies (or even universes), but it will also need to be considered how the narrative framing conditions these questions. William Mayne's *The Blemyah Stories* (1987), intriguingly illustrated by Juan Wijngaard, is another fertile source.

Finally, parodies or re-versions can function as carnivalesque, interrogative discourses. Needle's *Wild Wood* (1981) is a significant modern example.

FURTHER READING

Studies of the carnivalesque inevitably begin with Bakhtin (1965); children's fiction has not previously been examined from this perspective, though pertinent insights may be extrapolated from Bristol (1985) and especially LaCapra (1983, Chapters 1 and 9). For carnival as a transgressive force, see White (1982). Katz (1980) is a good discussion of food in children's literature. For a study of subjectivity, gender and class in schools, see Walkerdine (1985).

FIVE

Primary scenes: the family and picture books

The concern of this chapter is with ways in which picture books deal with ideological practices operating as interactions between members of a family group. The family is the first social structure with which children interact, and usually the first contact a child has with books is with picture books, which remain the principal literary form up to and beyond the age at which children master literacy for themselves. Picture books can, of course, exist for fun, but they can never be said to exist without either a socializing or educational intention, or else without a specific orientation towards the reality constructed by the society that produces them. The latter point hardly needs making, but is nevertheless easy to overlook. In order to make sense to its viewers, a picture book will be grounded in some version of consensus reality and use conventional codes of representation. Yet in various ways both of these things have to be learned, as a child learns about the social formations of its immediate and then more distant context (immediate and extended family structures, for example), and about the codes by which these are visually represented, as dress, gesture, and so on. Viewers thus have to learn how to interpret or 'read' a picture just as much as a verbal text, and that learning is part of acculturation. It is merely sentimental to assert that children see with unspoiled perceptions and therefore see everything in a scene, whereas corrupted adult perceptions see only in part because they ignore minor details. As Nodelman points out, visual representations cannot be understood without 'a knowledge of learned competencies and cultural assumptions' (1988, p. 17). Thus one of the principal functions of books for babies is to begin training in visual literacy. This involves learning the conventions whereby actual world phenomena are represented – for example, in two dimensions, in stylized forms, close up or far away, and as seen from different positions.

Jan Pienkowski's 'Look at me' series offers an illuminating example. *I'm Mouse* (1985) aims to teach babies some basic concepts of spatial (specifically dimensional) orientation through a combination of simple verbal text and conventionally stylized pictures. The book is made from heavy cardboard, consists of four double-page spreads, and tells a simple story which nevertheless has to be inferred from the combination of text and pictures. In other words, it is a quite subtle and sophisticated text for babies. The verbal text is a single, fifteen-word 'sentence' extended throughout the book, and consists of an imperative clause – 'Look at me' – with four adjuncted prepositional phrases. The 'story' is about a mouse's journey across a room; the final picture offers the retrospective information that it was chased by a cat. The discourse performs a surprisingly large number of functions. It offers an incipiently verbal child practice in the manipulation of four dimensional prepositions ('up', 'down', 'under' and 'in'), and as it does that the appropriate orientations of 'up', 'down' and 'under' also imply that this book has to be held only one way up for that information to make sense. The mouse's passage from clock to mousehole teaches that events, and the books that encode events, have particular sequences. It teaches or reinforces (obviously enough) the information that the world contains mice and cats, and it is normal for the former to be chased by the latter. By attributing the narration to Mouse, the book begins to inculcate conventional attitudes towards certain animals which culminates in picture-book anthropomorphism. The discourse teaches that an object can be represented in a number of possible ways, by conventional features, and by minimal detail; in this case, the essential attributes of mouse-ness are a long tail and prominent rounded ears. In Figure 5:1, below, the re-drawing of the four representations of Mouse shows how conventional they are – anybody asked to sketch a mouse will usually reproduce a version of one of them. In each representation, tail and ears are larger than on an actual mouse. The infant audience is unlikely, perhaps, ever to have seen a mouse, but that is hardly to the point, since what is being learned is one picture-book convention for how mice appear. The four illustrations thus also function like a draughtsman's plan: (1) profile in action; (3) profile at rest; (2) superior view; and (4) rear view. Further, (3) includes a comment on object permanence by showing part of the tail concealed by the leg of the bed, and (4) demonstrates how shift in point of view functions, since the audience is situated behind the mouse inside the mouse-

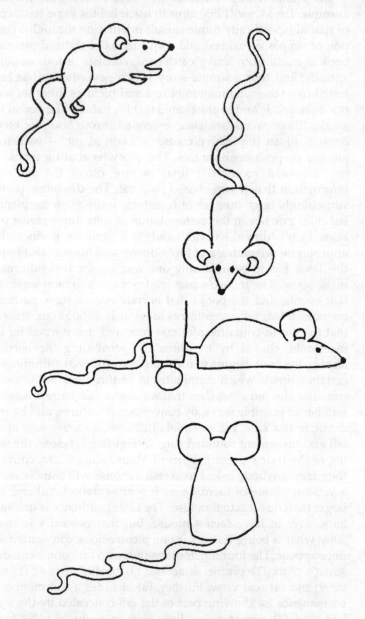

Figure 5:1 Representations of 'Mouse'

hole looking out at part of a cat's head. This shift in point of view has the further implication that the audience can take up more than one subject position, looking first *at* mouse and later *with* mouse, though the effect of this here is to enact the transfer from an observer subject position to identification with a small and threatened creature, a position frequently constructed for child audiences. Yet another lesson in representation taught by this book is that objects can be represented in part only: a quarter of the clock; stripes for the curtains (unidentifiable without the text); half the bed; half the cat's face (geometric shapes – semicircles and triangles of red, yellow and green – suggesting head, eye, ear). It would be safe to say that the book's target audience could not identify the cat as such, but there is also an exercise here in simple intertextuality, since if the baby also possesses the companion book *I'm Cat* she may be able to recognize that these shapes (and colours) depict the same cat here.

There are thus a large number of negotiations which the audience must carry out on encountering this book, and these will initially need to be traversed with guidance from the adult who performs the text. I have merely summarized those operations here; for a fuller discussion of some of the issues of representation involved see Nodelman's *Words About Pictures* (1988, pp. 21–35). *I'm Mouse* is about as neutral as one can get, in that most of its processes are directed towards developing expertise in language and in interpreting visual images, though the potential for manipulation of perception and construction of particular subject positions through its various processes is quite evident.

Reading even a simple picture book is thus quite a complex cognitive process. Audiences not only need to be able to decode the verbal text – its grammar, its syntax, its semantic structures, and so on – but also need to develop an understanding of how to 'read' a picture in terms of the conventions by which it operates. But having grasped some basic principles, a small child may be able to engage more imaginatively with a picture's conventional or mimetic representation of appearances than with a text for which she may have insufficient linguistic experience. Text and picture can strongly reinforce one another, as in *I'm Mouse*, expanding perceptions both of language and of the world. But very many contemporary picture books operate the other way round, having simple and even artless texts, or sometimes no text at all, but very sophisticated and highly accomplished pictures. As purported representations of the actual world, pictures can powerfully inscribe both explicit and implicit ideologies.

As was implicit in my comments on *I'm Mouse*, pictures, like verbal texts, can be discussed in terms of their discourse, story and significance, since they too have a 'what' and a 'how' made up of represented objects and a mode or style of representation. Further, as all texts carry within them attitudes and ideologies, so also do pictures: we cannot respond to them objectively, since they arouse emotional responses perhaps more quickly than they do intellectual ones, but in any case do both because a representation of something is always at the same time an *interpretation* of it. Point of view, which so far I have stressed principally with relation to verbal texts, can become absolutely crucial in pictures. This means, firstly, point of view in the literal sense of where the viewer is positioned in relation to the picture, since although we are always in front of it the artist can exploit perspective to create the illusion that we are above the scene, or beneath it, or off to one side: such a strategy effects significance by, say, foregrounding some particular sector of the picture. Secondly, the picture may represent the point of view of a figure within the picture itself, so that we, the viewers, either see from the same vantage point as that focalizing figure, or, seeing from a different vantage point, we see a different scene which includes within it a figure seeing. This enables the viewer to construct quite complex subject positions, being able at once to assess the perspective of the focalizing figure within the picture and to remain separate from that focalization. Thirdly, we can speak of 'point of view' in the sense of an attitude expressed or evoked, and in pictures, I think, this is a secondary effect arising out of the previous uses: that is to say, it is a matter of such things as thematic significances which arise out of discourse. The final audience subject position in *I'm Mouse* illustrates this third kind of point of view.

Before turning to some picture books about families, I want to consider the mode of signification in another book for a very young audience, Pat Hutchins' modern classic, *Rosie's Walk*. Once again, the apparent object of the verbal text is to teach dimensional prepositions, though now this is more heavily subordinated to a narrative interest. The text is again a single sentence, this time consisting of two correlative clauses which function formally as the *beginning* and *end* of a narrative sequence, as marked by the semantic relationship of the two verbs which frame it, 'went' and 'got back'. The *middle* of the narrative is made up of a series of prepositional phrases adjuncted to the first clause. It is a very minimal narrative, and at text level is hardly more than the lesson in the use of six dimensional prepositions ('across', 'around', 'over', 'past', 'through' and 'under'), which the pictures do indeed illustrate. But because of the way the pictures relate to that simple text, the book becomes a fascinating, exciting and amusing experience. The pictures make it a fuller narrative by laying out a scene around the words, making them both more specific and creating meaningful contexts for them, but they also encourage a more complex response to the text. Pictures can reveal things that the words do not, and their interesting details are clues to a more interesting story than the one the words tell. The distance between pictures and words can function as comedy or irony, and this can even be at the expense of the narrator, as seems to be the case with *Rosie's Walk*.

A picture is a frozen moment in time, not subject to the demands of forward motion which control the verbal text. This is obvious from the opening spread of *Rosie's Walk*. We can enter the picture at any point, and if we happen to be a young child not yet trained to interpret books from left to right, we might well start anywhere; but in fact the text carefully orients the viewer's gaze by drawing attention to Rosie and to the information that she is going for a walk. Rosie is situated slightly off-centre, but her narrative centrality is reinforced because the objects at the edges of the picture (buildings, cart, fox) are incomplete; the picture co-operates with the text in that Rosie is depicted in a stance which conventionally denotes 'walking', i.e. one foot flat on the ground (heel and toe), one uplifted. The picture is a very flat profile: while there are minimal attempts at perspective in the drawing of the buildings, the milk cans and the cart are 'flat', with no attempt to suggest three-dimensionality. The scene is also presented at the same 'height' as the viewer, who is positioned full frontal to it. This encourages the viewer to seek the linearity implied by 'a walk' – where is Rosie going? Where has she come from? The important addition in the illustration, which will prove to function in counterpoint with the text, is the presence of the fox. Throughout the book the fox makes a series of bumbled attempts to catch the hen, but these are registered neither by the hen nor the narrating text. Thus on the next double page the fox pounces; the text merely states that Rosie walked across the yard, but the picture shows both the pouncing and the setting up of the old slap-stick gag about treading on the head of a rake, and on the next page again, which is wordless, we see the fox discomfited.

The audience's encounter with the book is thus again very complex. First, the book introduces its audience to an important principle of intelligent picture books, a capacity to construct and exploit a contradiction between text and picture so that the two complement one another and together produce a story and a significance that depend on their differences from each other. Further, because individual pictures do not have grammar, syntax or linear flow, but freeze specific moments in time, rarely presenting more than one event within a single frame, this relationship between text and picture is one between differently constructed discourses giving different kinds of information, if not different messages. Hence the audience will experience a complicated process of decoding, so that a text which by itself is a series of inconsequential events structured as a language lesson, and as such might be expected to strive for clarity and precise, single meaning, becomes only a surface beneath which other kinds of meaning can be perceived, and meaningfulness itself becomes problematic. At the same time, the audience is being offered three different ways of relating to the book: he may be a superior subject, a cooperative subject, or a subjected subject, depending on the answer to the following questions. Is the narrating voice as oblivious as Rosie to the fox's presence? Is the narrator in collusion with the audience, sharing a joke about the story? Or is the narrator teasing the audience?

What, finally, does *Rosie's Walk* tell us about the world? One of its functions is to teach/reinforce a social concept of humour. Treading on rakes, being covered in flour, being caught in runaway vehicles, or being chased by bees are not intrinsically funny events. It is a learned social convention that such events can be regarded as funny, and we learn the situations in which this applies. The ironical counterpoint of text and pictures constitutes these events as comic, even if the audience has not yet learned to recognize them as such. More specifically, comic villains may readily suffer such mishaps. It renders them less threatening, but also, especially when such accidents occur within a narrative sequence and are linked in a cause-and-effect relationship to attempted acts of villainy, as in *Rosie's Walk*, it implies that evil brings about its own undoing. This is a tenet that has become deeply ingrained in children's literature, especially in fantasy, and must be seen as an element motivating the recent genre of pessimistic realism. It is already being learned from *Rosie's Walk*. Rosie simply passes through her world in quiet self-absorption and unknowingly avoids its major threat. Her escape may seem merely a matter of chance, and she herself may seem incredibly stupid, which offers one way of reading her obliviousness to danger. But nevertheless her implicit passivity may also represent a chosen quietude, and hence an ideological construct crucial for how we think about society and for how we envisage engagement with it or separation from it. Either way, it is an ideological issue that cannot simply be ignored.

Picture books express a wide range of ideological positions – some explicit, some implicit, some affirming dominant social apparatuses, some challenging, as I showed in Chapter 4. For the rest of this chapter I will be examining three groupings of picture books. I have put them together on a thematic basis, usually linking books which contrast ideologically. Those I have chosen are mostly family-centred, and most have transposed their representations of human society into anthropomorphic animal stories. I have selected widely across the publishing spectrum to include both mass-market books, such as Little Golden Books, and the more expensive 'quality' books. It would require a study in itself to determine convincingly if there are ideological differences between these groups, and this would need to consider such factors as date of production, country of origin and class affiliations of the envisaged market, but amongst those I have analysed the tendency seems to be for mass market books to construct more socially conservative outcomes and to confirm parental authority within the family hierarchy. The discussion below will be principally concerned with the representation of family structures and of social and narrative processes, especially point of view and subject position.

SIBLING RIVALRY

The development of a close bond between children of the same family is an ideal which lies at the heart of much social practice. Harmony and disharmony between brothers and sisters is an age-old story motif. It pervades folk and fairy story (*Cinderella; Beauty and the Beast; The Three Feathers;* the Bible story of Joseph and his brothers; and so on), and informs the figurative language commonly used to signify wider social, national and international relations. It is apt to be of interest to any child with one or more siblings, and the theme is also a site upon which authors can begin to build the themes of social integration of larger kinds, especially since the presence of an Other within a child's most immediate group constitutes a major assault on infantile solipsism, self-absorption and selfishness. I will here discuss some books which advance two solutions to sibling rivalry, one parent-controlled and the other peer-resolved.

(1) Parental interventions

This section will be concerned with two books, produced a quarter of a century apart, which deal with the negative responses of an older sister towards the introduction into the family of a younger sibling, offering reassurance to the older child that she is still important to the family and has privileges and even responsibilities as the older child. The books are Joan Elizabeth Goodman's, *The Bears' New Baby* (1988), and Russell and Lillian Hoban's, *A Baby Sister for Frances* (1964). The message conveyed by these books is essentially the same, though is expressed more directly and emphatically in the more recent one. Each book depicts a nuclear family, though one is a family of bears and the other of badgers. The Goodman, in particular, is intensely anthropomorphic, since the bear-characters live, dress, speak, eat and generally behave like humans, and are very humanoid in appearance. The Hobans' book is more ambiguously anthropomorphic: the mother badger wears a skirt and apron (in other books in the *Frances*-series, she wears a neck-to-ankle dress); the father wears glasses, but no clothes, and smokes a pipe; Frances dresses to go to school (as elsewhere in the series), but not at other times or for other activities. In neither book do the characters exhibit any traces of animal behaviour, but are surrogate humans in all respects.

Amanda, the main character of *The Bears' New Baby* is essentially solipsistic, seeing the family as existing for the sake of her self. Thus she greets the prospect of a sibling enthusiastically at first, planning to name it 'Wiggles', and anticipating 'how much fun she would have with Wiggles' (Goodman, *The Bears' New Baby*, p. 5). That is, she interprets the situation in terms of her own power and pleasure. The exploration of her desires and responses is carried out by means of a narrative strategy which epitomizes a method by which a text can construct a reader subject position which is in fact a *sub-*

jected position. As the text's focalizing child-figure, Amanda invites reader identification. But the story is also presented largely through conversation which consistently disempowers Amanda, and suggests a reader position that identifies many of Amanda's thoughts and responses as 'childish' rather than child-like. The following exchange is a simple example:

> Mama's tummy grew bigger and bigger. Amanda could feel the baby move inside.
> 'It keeps moving around,' said Amanda. 'I'm going to call it Wiggles.'
> 'Wiggles is a good name for a baby,' said Mama. 'Let's think of grown-up names, too . . .
>
> (Goodman, *The Bears' New Baby*, p. 4)

The focalization is clear from the indication of child-language in the 'cute' narrative register, most obvious in 'Mama's tummy grew bigger and bigger' with its accretion of diminutives and naive repetition (the worst kind of writing for children, needless to say). Focalization is also marked by *inquit*-tags attached to other characters – Mama, Papa, Grandma – which identify them by their relationships to Amanda. The interplay of focalization and conversation dominance means that the mother's subtle put-down of the child in their speech exchange is, as it were, invisible to the character and quite possibly also not consciously registered by child audiences. The two parts of Amanda's utterance are linked causally and semantically through 'moving' and 'Wiggles', but the two parts of the mother's are disjunctive, as the semantic opposition of 'baby::grown-up' undermines the conjunctive effect of the repetition in 'name::names'. A less obvious effect is the subsidiary opposition of the parallel qualifiers 'good::grown-up' (discreetly emphasized by the alliteration). This socially complex situation, offering positive approbation to the child while maintaining a negative practical position, reflects a strategy which is a normal part of adult–child exchanges. Again, it is hard to know whether the strategy will be recognized or silently internalized by child audiences. In either case the audience is being prompted to condescend towards their own childishness.

There are very few directive cues to accompany the conversation. Only one *inquit*-tag is qualified, and that by an accompanying action ('giving Amanda a big hug', p. 11), and none is semantically loaded; the only *inquit*-tags employed are 'said', 'asked' and 'thought' (with, once, 'felt' introducing indirect thought). This limited group is, nevertheless, more varied than in the Hoban, which employs an unvaried 'said' as the only tag, reflecting the absence there of developed character focalization. Further, the exchanges between child and adults in *The Bears' New Baby* consist mainly of question–answer pairs. Thus of twenty-six utterances made by Amanda, thirteen are interrogatives and thirteen declaratives. Only Amanda's utterances are tagged by 'asked' or 'thought' – the latter because, as sole focalizer, she is the only character to whose mind the audience is given access. Moreover, Amanda's declaratives tend to be complaints. The following sequence illustrates a central aspect of the process:

> 'When will he be big enough to play with me?' she asked.
> 'Soon,' said Mama. 'In the meantime, Wiggles will keep us very busy.'
> 'Wiggles certainly keeps Mama busy,' thought Amanda as the days went by.
>
> (Goodman, *The Bears' New Baby*, pp. 13–14)

Amanda's questions generally fail to elicit a precise response, and the reply 'soon' points to a second theme in the book, the inculcation of patience as a virtue, so that by the final page, when the baby at last has begun to learn to play, 'soon' has been recuperated for Amanda so that she can make a joke about it. Secondly, the semantic drift between the two occurrences of 'busy' in the extract marks the child's re-encoding of the mother's attempt at explanation into a covert complaint. The direction tends rather to go the other way, however, in that the question–answer dialogue usually marks a parental recognition of the child's viewpoint and an attempt to modify it:

> 'Wiggles is not the kind of baby I wanted,' said Amanda. 'Couldn't we send him back?'
> 'No,' said Papa. 'Besides, soon Wiggles will be bigger and more fun to play with. Then, I think, you will like him very much.'
> 'Soon, hmph!' said Amanda. 'I don't think Wiggles will *ever* get bigger or be *any* fun!'
> 'But he gets bigger all the time!' said Papa. 'You must watch him more carefully.'
>
> (Goodman, *The Bears' New Baby*, pp. 15–16)